CHRIST'S
MILLENNIAL
KINGDOM

Published by Amazon KDP

Cover design: Jessica Quinton
Typesetting: Plantin Light

ISBN: 978-3-63446-747-0

CHRIST'S MILLENNIAL KINGDOM

The Great Hope of Mankind

Jessica Quinton

Acknowledgements

With heartfelt thanks to my dear Granny for her spiritual
encouragement and assistance with editing this book.
Thank you also to my wonderful parents for their helpful input
and loving support.

Contents

Daniel 7:13-14

"I was watching in the night visions, and behold, One like the Son of Man, coming with the clouds of heaven! He came to the Ancient of Days, and they brought Him near before Him.

Then to Him was given dominion and glory and a kingdom, that all peoples, nations, and languages should serve Him. His dominion is an everlasting dominion, which shall not pass away, and His kingdom the one which shall not be destroyed."

Introduction

I have always been fascinated by thoughts of what is to come. The prospects of my future excite me. Perhaps that is what first drew me to study such a vast topic as Christ's Millennial Kingdom.

When reading through my Bible recently, I noticed a theme that kept sticking out to me, as if highlighted on the pages. Verses I hadn't given much notice before came alive to me, resonating deep within. A hope was birthed within me for the future of those who love God, and for what the Lord has planned for His people as a whole. I collated these verses and categorized them for my own study, creating a backbone for the following chapters, although I did not know it at the time.

The theme catching my attention was the time period between the return of Jesus, and the creation of a new heaven and earth: Christ's one-thousand-year rule. Did you know that in the Old Testament, there are more prophecies about the Millennial Kingdom and second coming of Jesus, than there are of His first coming? The scriptures point towards a period of time in the future where Christ will physically rule on earth as King, along with His people. It is perhaps one of the most fascinating and beautiful promises found in God's word. No mind can imagine the glory prepared for those who love the Lord!

There are hundreds of incredible prophecies written, that are yet to be fulfilled. Scripture tells us that the Messiah will rule physically on earth from a temple in Jerusalem – this is yet to come! His word declares that the lost tribes of Israel (those which are currently still scattered throughout the earth) will be brought back to the Promised Land – this is yet to come! All will bow to Jesus. Martyrs will resurrect. Believers will be exalted. This is just a fraction of what is to take place at the second coming of Christ! And these things have clearly not yet taken place.

There are two major prophetic pictures described in the Bible that revolve around Israel: the Millennial Kingdom and the New Jerusalem. Whilst similar, they take place at completely different times. The Millennial Kingdom will last for 1000 years on earth after the return of Christ, whereas the New Jerusalem will be established after judgement day when all the dead have been resurrected, and will continue for eternity. When finding verses for this book, I was careful to distinguish between the two time periods to make my writing as accurate as possible. Whilst the lines appeared blurred in some prophecies, it was almost always easy to tell the subject matter by reading through the wider context of the verses.

One of the major prophecies marking the start of the Millennial Kingdom, is the return of the children of God to the land of Israel - the land flowing with milk and honey, promised to Abraham and his descendants. The Bible refers collectively to God's people as 'Israel', and as such I have adopted the same terminology in my writing. Israel is the term used by God to describe His chosen people, His followers. It does not necessarily refer to the people who are currently dwelling within that holy land, unless they have made Jesus King of their lives. Therefore, the word 'Israel' can be interchangeable with 'God's people' or even 'us' if you are a child of God. Making this our perspective changes the way we look at these scriptures, reminding us that these verses are actually written about us! They are relevant and vitally important to us as believers.

Let the following chapters inspire you with hope for our futures. We are God's most precious people, and the plans that He has for us are incredible! I pray that God will unravel a deeper knowledge of the things He has in store for you, my friends.

Chapter 1

The Millennial Kingdom as Seen in the Book of Revelation

The Millennial Kingdom is a period of a thousand years in the future, when Christ will rule on earth. The Bible tells us that with the return of Jesus, the children of God will be gathered from all the nations of the earth and dwell in Zion. Here, Christ will rule and reign over the earth from His holy temple, before the day of judgement and final resurrection. It is exciting to think this could happen within our lifetimes, but if not, we can be excited for the generation of people who do get to witness it! There are great visions of the Millennial Kingdom in Revelation, and descriptions of it from several Old-Testament prophets including Isaiah, Ezekiel, Zephaniah, Zechariah and Malachi.

John's vision in Revelation gives a timeline of end time events, providing an interesting insight into the Millennial Kingdom and how it fits into the events that surround it. Just before the start of the Millenium, Jesus Christ returns to the earth in great glory and splendour, as described in Revelation 19:11-16:

'Now I saw heaven opened, and behold, a white horse. And He who sat on him was called Faithful and True, and in righteousness He judges and makes war. His eyes were like a flame of fire, and on His head were many crowns. He had a name written that no one knew except Himself. He was clothed with a robe dipped in blood, and His name is called The Word of God. And the armies in heaven, clothed in fine linen, white and clean, followed Him on white horses. Now out of His mouth goes a sharp sword, that with it He should strike the nations. And He Himself will rule them with a rod of iron. He Himself treads the winepress of the fierceness and wrath of Almighty God. And He has on His robe and on His thigh a name written: KING OF KINGS AND LORD OF LORDS.'

What an incredible picture! The King of all the earth will come down, in the perfect appearance of holiness, righteousness and lordship. He will arrive riding on a white horse with many crowns upon His head, a sword protruding from His mouth, and His eyes burning like flames of fire. All the armies of heaven will follow him in clean robes and will also ride on white horses. What a majestic and fearsome sight - He is coming to save his people and to destroy the works of the evil one!

Following on from this, Revelation 20:1-10 details a fascinating list of events, starting with the locking up of Satan, and ending with the judgement day. The Millennial Kingdom occurs between these two.

Revelation 20:1-3 – 'Then I saw an angel coming down from heaven, having the key to the bottomless pit and a great chain in his hand. He laid hold of the dragon, that serpent of old, who is the Devil and Satan, and bound him for a thousand years; and he cast him into the bottomless pit, and shut him up, and set a seal on him, so that he should deceive the nations no more till the thousand years were finished. But after these things he must be released for a little while.'

What an incredible time it will be when Satan is bound by an angel and sealed in the bottomless pit for a thousand years! What a celebration it will cause. The devil will not be able to deceive the world at all during this time, and after his release, he will only be able to do so for a short time. Evil and suffering therefore will be completely stalled during this one-thousand-year period. The vision continues:

Revelation 20:4-6 – 'And I saw thrones, and they sat on them, and judgment was committed to them. Then I saw the souls of those who had been beheaded for their witness to Jesus and for the word of God, who had not worshiped the beast or his image, and had not received his mark on their foreheads or on their hands. And they lived and reigned with Christ for a thousand years. But the rest of the dead did not live again until the thousand years were finished. This is the first resurrection. Blessed and holy is he who has part in the first resurrection. Over such the second death has no power, but they shall be priests of God and of Christ, and shall reign with Him a thousand years.'

At the return of Jesus, there will be a resurrection of all martyrs who have died for Him on earth, along with those who have refused to worship the antichrist during his rule. For the full one thousand years, these resurrected ones will reign with Christ and be seated on thrones in his Kingdom, being granted the authority to judge the nations. What an incredible reward! Surely, the trials and persecution we face in life are nothing compared to the glory and honour of what is to come, as said by Paul (**Romans 8:18**). Anyone who is not in this category will remain in their graves until after the one thousand years, at the time of the second resurrection.

Next, John's vision briefly describes the period after the one-thousand-year rule, as written below:

Revelation 20:7-10 – 'Now when the thousand years have expired, Satan will be released from his prison and will go out to deceive the nations which are in the four corners of the earth, Gog and Magog, to gather them together to battle, whose number is as the sand of the sea. They went up on the breadth of the earth and surrounded the camp of the saints and the beloved city. And fire came down from God out of heaven and devoured them. The devil, who deceived them, was cast into the lake of fire and brimstone where the beast and the false prophet are. And they will be tormented day and night forever and ever.'

Satan will be released from his binding, and will deceive the world as before, but only for a set time. Although we are not told exactly how long this will be, we are promised it will be short. During this time, Satan will gather an army from across the world to fight alongside him in battle, and together they will surround Jerusalem, ready to attack. Satan desires to conquer the city of God, and to take ownership of the earth, but there is no such hope for him. Before the battle even begins, God will send fire from heaven to consume every part of his evil army. The Lord makes sure that no harm is done to His chosen people, protecting them with His strength and fury. Straight after this, the devil is thrown into the lake of fire and brimstone where he will be tormented for eternity, along with the end times' beast and false prophet who had been deceiving the world before the coming of Christ. Evil will never prevail against the righteous power of God.

Once Satan has been removed, the day of judgement will arrive:

Revelation 20:11-13 – 'Then I saw a great white throne and Him who sat on it, from whose face the earth and the heaven fled away. And there was found no place for them. And I saw the dead, small and great, standing before God, and books were opened. And another book was opened, which is the Book of Life. And the dead were judged according to their works, by the things which were written in the books. The sea gave up the dead who were in it, and Death and Hades delivered up the dead who were in them. And they were judged, each one according to his works.'

All people will be raised from the dead in this second resurrection and will stand together before the throne of God. The greatness of God will be so astounding and terrifying that even heaven and earth will flee away. With every human that ever lived standing before God, the books that contain all our deeds and actions are opened so that we may be judged according to how we have lived. This is a frightening thought, but one that should be kept as a constant reality in our minds. On this day, some will rise to everlasting life, and some will rise to everlasting condemnation. God is righteous, and His judgement is perfect.

After judgement is complete, a new heaven and earth is created to replace the old, and eternity begins. The glory of eternity will be even greater than the glory of the Millennial Kingdom, and the righteous will be given new and perfect bodies, no longer marked by sin or sadness. A New Jerusalem descends to earth, filled with God's people – the beautiful bride of Christ. The city will be transformed from what it was in the Millennial Kingdom – it will be made of pure gold, with walls of jasper, gates of pearls and foundations made with twelve types of precious stones. No temple will be there, for God's presence will be our temple. No darkness or night will be present, for God will be our light.

Revelation 21:3-4 – 'And I heard a loud voice from the throne saying, "Look! God's dwelling place is now among the people, and he will dwell with them. They will be his people, and God himself will be with them and be their God. 'He will wipe every tear from their eyes. There will be no more death' or mourning or crying or pain, for the old order of things has passed away."'

Hallelujah!

Chapter 2

God's Promises to Abraham and Israel's Disobedience

To fully grasp the wonder of the Millennial Kingdom and the future of Jerusalem, it is first important to look back on Israel's past and to the promises given to Abraham, Isaac, and Jacob, which still hold true today. These promises are among the most tremendous in the Bible, their weight everlasting and their blessings remaining true from generation to generation. In Genesis 12:1-3, the Lord speaks to Abraham for the first time, declaring:

"Get out of your country, from your family and from your father's house, to a land that I will show you. I will make you a great nation; I will bless you and make your name great; and you shall be a blessing. I will bless those who bless you, and I will curse him who curses you; and in you all the families of the earth shall be blessed."

Abraham was being told to leave his family and the comfort of everything that he knew, full of faith for the Promised Land God had prepared for him, putting all his confidence in the Lord. If Abraham were to obey (which thankfully he did), he would receive all that was promised to him in the following verses. What

God said here must have been incredible for Abraham to hear – almost too great to bear. He himself would become the father of a great nation. At this stage, Abraham did not even have children and was seventy five years of age! The promise that a nation would arise from him was not only astounding, but also miraculous. Following this, God blesses Abraham and declares that all the families of the earth would be blessed through him. I believe much of this promise will be fulfilled when Israel once again becomes glorified in the days of Christ's reign on earth. However, it has already been fulfilled in part through Abraham's great bloodline, and through the life-giving scriptures we can study because of his family and their obedience to God.

Time and time again God expands upon His promises to Abraham, adding new wonders for him to meditate upon. In Genesis 13:14-17, God says to Abraham after Lot had gone his separate way:

"Lift your eyes now and look from the place where you are-- northward, southward, eastward, and westward; for all the land which you see I give to you and your descendants forever. And I will make your descendants as the dust of the earth; so that if a man could number the dust of the earth, then your descendants also could be numbered. Arise, walk in the land through its length and its width, for I give it to you."

The image of greatness, vastness and eternity completely encompasses these verses. In every direction Abraham looked, he could see the land that God promised would be his. And not only land for himself, but for all his descendants forevermore. What an amazing gift! God encourages Abraham to walk 'through its length and its width', familiarising himself with it and letting the words of God sink into his heart and mind. Just as it was with Abraham, it is important for us to metaphorically 'walk in the land through its length and its width', by familiarising ourselves with the promises that God has for our lives and our futures. We need to do this so that we are prepared to settle in His promises, being able to receive the inheritance that God has waiting for us. We need to be a people who are ready and prepared. One reason I decided to write on this subject, was for an opportunity to meditate deeply on the promises and prophecies that God has given us throughout the Bible. We can be sure these will take place either in our lifetimes, our descendants' lifetimes, or both. God's promises should become our treasured possessions.

Another declaration for Abraham to grasp hold of and believe, was that his descendants would be numbered as the dust of the earth. This promise must have been astounding to hear, and something Abraham may have come close to doubting, firstly when he had no children and later when he was called to sacrifice his chosen son. However, we can see through scriptures that Abraham was obedient, being referred to as a friend of God in Isaiah 41:8. As a result of his obedience, he received the blessings of God's promises. Through Abraham's seed, Israel did indeed become a vast and conquering nation, defeating the ungodly peoples surrounding them to expand their God-given territory. It is estimated that 600,000 Israelites left their captivity in Egypt with Moses, and today millions of people must be descended from their bloodlines.

Even those who are not related by blood to Abraham today, are called to be part of Israel, God's chosen nation, if they are the Lord's children and born again of the Spirit. All believers have been joined together as one body of Christ, one church, one bride. This spiritual unity could not have been possible if not for the death of Jesus and His great love for us, dying for Jews and Gentiles alike. The following passage from Ephesians speaks to the Gentiles, explaining how they used to be far from Israel and God's promises, but now have been brought near:

Ephesians 2:12-13 – 'that at that time you were without Christ, being aliens from the commonwealth of Israel and strangers from the covenants of promise, having no hope and without God in the world. But now in Christ Jesus you who once were far off have been brought near by the blood of Christ.'

Because of the great love of the Father, all of God's children are now included under the bracket of Israel, regardless of race. Our inheritance is found in Him and what He promises us, so we too can celebrate the promises given to Abraham! We are part of a great and victorious nation. **Romans 9:6-8** reiterates this:

'For they are not all Israel who are of Israel, nor are they all children because they are the seed of Abraham; but, "In Isaac your seed shall be called." That is, those who are the children of the flesh, these are not the children of God; but the children of the promise are counted as the seed.'

These verses explain that not all of Abraham's physical descendants are true children of God – only those who follow God's ways. For example, the Pharisees (who were Jewish by race) were called children of Satan by Jesus, since they sought human approval over God's approval and therefore did not love God in their hearts. However, children of the promise (a term not limited to blood or relations) are counted as true 'seed' (descendants) of Abraham in God's eyes. Children of the promise includes us too if we have accepted Jesus as the King of our lives.

The promise of land and descendants continues throughout Genesis. Shortly after Abraham's death, Isaac receives this amazing statement from God:

Genesis 26:3-5 – "Dwell in this land, and I will be with you and bless you; for to you and your descendants I give all these lands, and I will perform the oath which I swore to Abraham your father. And I will make your descendants multiply as the stars of heaven; I will give to your descendants all these lands; and in your seed all the nations of the earth shall be blessed; because Abraham obeyed My voice and kept My charge, My commandments, My statutes, and My laws."

Speaking the same words to Isaac as spoken to his father, God confirms that these promises will last from generation to generation, the blessing everlasting. God is not only the God of Abraham, but He is the God of Isaac, Jacob and their descendants forevermore. He wants an intimate relationship with every one of the children of the promise and to bless each one personally. The reason for the blessing that God bestowed on Israel is given in the verses above – it was as a result of Abraham's obedience to God's voice, charge, commandments, statutes and laws. For each generation to come, it is essential that people obey God fully in order to inherit the promises given to our forefathers. This concept can be studied more fully through reading **Deuteronomy 28**, which begins by listing the blessings that would come to Israel if they obeyed the voice of God and ends with a warning of the curses that would come with disobeying His voice. In **Deuteronomy 28** Moses declares to the people,

28:1 – "If you fully obey the Lord your God and carefully follow all his commands I give you today, the Lord your God will set you high above all the nations on earth."

28:9 – "The Lord will establish you as his holy people, as he promised you on oath, if you keep the commands of the Lord your God and walk in obedience to him."

28:15 – "However, if you do not obey the Lord your God and do not carefully follow all his commands and decrees I am giving you today, all these curses will come on you and overtake you:"

28:36 – "The Lord will drive you and the king you set over you to a nation unknown to you or your ancestors. There you will worship other gods, gods of wood and stone."

28:43 – "The foreigners who reside among you will rise above you higher and higher, but you will sink lower and lower."

28:64 – "Then the Lord will scatter you among all nations, from one end of the earth to the other. There you will worship other gods—gods of wood and stone, which neither you nor your ancestors have known."

Carefully obeying God would lead to Israel becoming the greatest nation on the earth, a holy people set apart for God. Conversely, disobedience would cause the people of Israel to be scattered across the nations of the earth, where they would sink low in the eyes of God and man, and would worship idols. God's laws should have been reverently followed by Israel, but we can see that they were not.

Over time, with passing generations and new kings, Israel lost that once intimate relationship it had with God. The nation turned away from the Lord, disobeying Him and worshipping idols instead, ignoring the warnings they had been given. King Jeroboam (ruler of the northern tribes of Israel after King Solomon) did evil in the Lord's eyes, making moulded images and worshipping idols, forgetting the God of his fathers. Because of this, the Lord's anger went out against Israel, fulfilling the curses of disobedience spoken by Moses. In 1 Kings 14:15-16, the prophet Abijah speaks the word of the Lord to Jeroboam:

"For the Lord will strike Israel, as a reed is shaken in the water. He will uproot Israel from this good land which He gave to their fathers, and will scatter them beyond the River, because they have made their wooden images, provoking the Lord to anger. And He will give Israel up because of the sins of Jeroboam, who sinned and who made Israel sin."

No longer would the nation of Israel dwell in the land given to them by God - they would be uprooted from the place He had carefully planted and nurtured them. Because the people rejected God, He too rejected them.

After successive kings and generations of people who did evil, the northern 10 tribes of Israel were taken captive by the Assyrians and scattered throughout that empire, becoming the '10 lost tribes'. The Southern tribe of Judah (including Benjamin) was taken captive to Babylon for 70 years. The prophet Ezekiel had been sent to speak God's word to the capital of Judah, Jerusalem, warning them of their wrongdoing and God's coming wrath:

Ezekiel 22:1-3 – 'Moreover the word of the Lord came to me, saying, "Now, son of man, will you judge, will you judge the bloody city? Yes, show her all her abominations! Then say, 'Thus says the Lord God: "The city sheds blood in her own midst, that her time may come; and she makes idols within herself to defile herself."'

And to Israel, God spoke through Ezekiel saying:

Ezekiel 12:15-16 – "I will scatter you among the nations, disperse you throughout the countries, and remove your filthiness completely from you. You shall defile yourself in the sight of the nations; then you shall know that I am the Lord."

Because of the repeated sins of the Israelites and their idolatry, they became defiled and cursed. God declared He would scatter them across the countries of the earth, so that they would no longer be one nation. A disobedient people could not receive an inheritance which was promised only to obedient children of the living God.

But there is hope.

Chapter 3

The Promise of Israel's Return

Throughout the Old Testament, it is promised that God will bring back the remnant of His people from the nations of the earth, where they have been scattered. Israel will once again become a victorious nation, ruled by God as King. Ezekiel 37:21-23 says:

'Thus says the Lord God: "Surely I will take the children of Israel from among the nations, wherever they have gone, and will gather them from every side and bring them into their own land; and I will make them one nation in the land, on the mountains of Israel; and one king shall be king over them all; they shall no longer be two nations, nor shall they ever be divided into two kingdoms again. They shall not defile themselves anymore with their idols, nor with their detestable things, nor with any of their transgressions; but I will deliver them from all their dwelling places in which they have sinned, and will cleanse them. Then they shall be My people, and I will be their God.'

One day in the future when Christ returns, the Lord will bring back all His children from the countries where they have been exiled, leaving none behind. He will bring them to the land He promised Abraham and his descendants, and Israel will again be made one nation. The land will no longer be split into northern and southern kingdoms, as it was after the reign of King

Solomon. Forever they will remain in unity like this – God promises they will never again be split in two. How excellent it will be when God's people are together forevermore, no longer spread out in the midst of evil nations! And on the mountains of Israel, one King shall reign over them – King Jesus.

After bringing back His people, God will cleanse Israel from their sins so that they will become a pure and holy nation before Him. There are many verses throughout the Bible that refer to God cleansing His people, which I will discuss in more detail in a later chapter. Whilst a lot of these verses describe the purification process that we experience throughout the course of our lives (as God moulds us into the likeness of His righteousness), there are multiple passages that explicitly describe how He will refine Israel when He brings them back from the nations of the earth. This process will be very necessary to remove the sins of His people, who will have come from nations lacking the fear of God and delighting in evil.

After being refined, Israel will no longer defile herself with idols or practise sinful ways but will live as obedient subjects to the Lord. He shall be their God, and they shall be His people. How spectacular! This is how we were always designed to live our lives – in perfect harmony with our Creator, honouring Him in all that we do. We shall be set apart as His holy people.

The chapter continues:

Ezekiel 37:24-28 – "David My servant shall be king over them, and they shall all have one shepherd; they shall also walk in My judgments and observe My statutes, and do them. Then they shall dwell in the land that I have given to Jacob My servant, where your fathers dwelt; and they shall dwell there, they, their children, and their children's children, forever; and My servant David shall be their prince forever. Moreover I will make a covenant of peace with them, and it shall be an everlasting covenant with them; I will establish them and multiply them, and I will set My sanctuary in their midst forevermore. My tabernacle also shall be with them; indeed I will be their God, and they shall be My people. The nations also will know that I, the Lord, sanctify Israel, when My sanctuary is in their midst forevermore."

Israel will have one King over them for the duration of these one thousand years, in contrast to the ever-changing rulers of the past. Whilst in this scripture, the king is said to be David (and this could indeed be a possibility), it is most likely meant to be understood as the root of David - Jesus the Messiah. Multiple times through the scriptures, Jesus is referred to as the son of David, and many verses declare that Christ Himself will rule Israel during the Millennial Kingdom. The verses above tell us that the King will reign forever and ever, meaning He will reign even beyond the Millennial Kingdom years and into the eternity of New Jerusalem.

Not only will Jesus be their mighty, victorious King, but also their gentle, loving Shepherd. All through the scriptures Jesus is referred to as our Good Shepherd, and He is most famously described as such in **John 10** and **Psalm 23**. In the Millennial Kingdom, Jesus will nurture Israel, lead them, care for them, and bring them to green pastures and rest. God will make an everlasting covenant of peace with His people. How glorious! Truly, Jesus is our Prince of Peace.

Israel will once again walk in God's judgements and observe His statutes, following in the footsteps of Abraham. As discussed in the previous chapter, obedience to God is what brings about the blessings of God - without obedience there can never be blessing. Because Israel will remain obedient to God throughout the period of the Millennial Kingdom and follow His ways, God promises that they shall dwell in the land given to their forefathers forever. Never again will they be scattered across the nations. Israel's continued obedience to God in the Millennial Kingdom is, I believe, as a result of the cleansing process which God took them through after gathering them from the nations. Without the grace and love of God, Israel would not have been refined in this way, and therefore at some stage would fall back into sin and disobedience, walking away from God's blessing once again. But God is merciful, and through His purification He will help His people walk in His ways, following His commands.

In the Promised Land, God will once again establish His people and multiply them. Since war with other nations will not take place in the Millennial Kingdom (discussed in a further chapter), all of this increase in numbers must be due to the people having many children. Israel will be obedient to God's first command to mankind – 'be fruitful and multiply', and God will bless their families. In the Millennial Kingdom, people will still be in their mortal bodies and able to reproduce (with the exception of the resurrected martyrs) – it is only after the second resurrection on judgment day, that we will be given new bodies. God will once again restore His people as a great nation.

The Lord will be in their midst forever, and He shall place His tabernacle in Israel. Yahweh shall be their God, and they shall be His people. The relationship between God and mankind, lost at the fall due to the sin of Adam and Eve, will once again be restored, and God will make His home among men. This is incredible! It is what our hearts long for. Our souls will find perfect fulfilment and rest in the presence of our King who will reign over us, shepherding us on earth. And all the surrounding nations shall know that God resides with His people, Israel. They shall see that Yahweh is Lord.

In Ezekiel 20:42 , God says:

"Then you shall know that I am the Lord, when I bring you into the land of Israel, into the country for which I raised My hand in an oath to give to your fathers."

Once God's children return to the land of Israel, all shall know that the Lord truly is God. His promises always come to pass, and His words never return void (Isaiah 55:11). Unfulfilled promises could never come from the true, living God. Yahweh swore an oath to Abraham, Isaac and Jacob declaring that the land He had shown them would be given to them and their descendants forever. Once Israel inherits the land promised to their fathers and dwells there forever, the oath will be complete, and all will know that it truly is Yahweh who is King, Creator and Lord.

The return of God's people was even prophesied by David, in **Psalm 14:7**:

'Oh, that the salvation of Israel would come out of Zion! When the Lord brings back the captivity of His people, Let Jacob rejoice and Israel be glad.'

This is simply amazing coming from David. Whilst he was king, Israel was still living in the land God had sworn to Abraham, and Israel was still one kingdom, not divided in two. In a single verse therefore, David prophesies both the scattering of Israel across the nations where they are sent into captivity, and their return when God draws them back together! He also sheds light on the joy and gladness of Israel as they return.

God is remarkable in the way He unravels His mysteries and future events to His people. There are so many key prophetic words like this in the Bible, waiting to be picked out and studied. We need to be aware of what God is telling us about our future.

Chapter 4

Who Will Enter the Promised Land?

We have seen that God's children will be gathered back to Israel, both Jews and Gentiles alike. It is important to understand though, that only a certain group of people are included in the bracket of God's children – only a remnant of Israel shall return.

Isaiah 10:21-22 – 'The remnant will return, the remnant of Jacob, to the Mighty God. For though your people, O Israel, be as the sand of the sea, a remnant of them will return; the destruction decreed shall overflow with righteousness.'

The literal seed of Abraham – the number of his descendants on earth at this time – will be as great in number as the sand of the sea. However, it is stated here that only a portion of these people will return to their Mighty God in the land that He has prepared for them. Who, therefore, will this remnant be? Who are the true children of God? The verse below uncovers answers to some of these questions.

Psalm 24:3-4 – 'Who may ascend into the hill of the Lord? Or who may stand in His holy place? He who has clean hands and a pure heart, who has not lifted up his soul to an idol, nor sworn deceitfully.'

The hill of the Lord is mentioned multiple times in the scriptures. It refers to Mount Zion, upon which the City of David is built, and will be the most holy place in the Millennial Kingdom, from where the Messiah will reign. In this Psalm, David is asking the Lord who is to be included in the assembly gathered at Zion during His rule. He then receives revelation from God in answer to this, which is written for us to read. Those that shall inherit the land of Israel during the Millennial Kingdom are the people who have clean hands and pure hearts. They will not have partaken in idol worship and will not have lived in deceit. Clean hands represent good deeds and actions: it is those who live righteously and flee from evil, who inherit the Promised Land. Having a pure heart implies pure thoughts, intentions and emotions. In Matthew 5:8, Jesus says:

"Blessed are the pure in heart, for they shall see God."

This consolidates the words of the psalmist – those who maintain purity, guarding their hearts, shall stand in God's holy place upon Mount Zion. Jesus proclaimed this as part of the Beatitudes, which were spoken to the disciples on a mountainside. During this talk, Jesus also declares that it is the poor in spirit (Matt 5:3) and those who are persecuted for righteousness' sake (Matt 5:10), who will receive the kingdom of heaven. It will be the meek that inherit the earth (Matt 5:5). The values of God's kingdom are somewhat opposite to the world's value system. The pure and humble, who rely fully on God and His righteousness in this life, are those who will be exalted in the end days, receiving the glorious inheritance of His Promised Land and Kingdom.

Doing good deeds and maintaining purity will never be enough on its own though. People will only be able to enter the kingdom of God through faith in Jesus, being confident that His blood shed on the cross was enough to cover all our sins. Jesus declares in John 14:6:

"I am the way, the truth, and the life. No one comes to the Father except through Me."

Humans can never become righteous through their own ability. We are sinful by nature due to the curse of the fall after man's first sin. It is only through the grace of God therefore, that we can be cleansed from the evil ways of our flesh and partake in God's holiness. Jesus paid the price for all our sins when He died upon the cross, and through His resurrection, we too have power over sin and death. We must have faith in the saving power of Christ's blood, and believe that through Him, we are able to renew our spirits in the likeness of His righteousness. Without faith in the power of His blood, we prevent Him from forgiving and refining us, and therefore we remain unrighteous in the sight of the Father and unworthy of the inheritance He has promised to His children. This is why it is only through Jesus – our only source of truth and life – that we can be saved.

Only those who trust in The Lord will enter Israel, when God draws them back from the nations.

Isaiah 57:13 – "When you cry out, let your collection of idols deliver you. But the wind will carry them all away, a breath will take them. But he who puts his trust in Me shall possess the land, and shall inherit My holy mountain."

Here, God is warning the Israelites that those who worship and trust in idols will not be delivered, whereas those who place their trust completely in Him will have total security, inheriting the Promised Land.

Similarly, **Revelation 20** reveals that those who die for the cause of Christ in their lifetime, and those who refuse to engage in idolatrous worship of the Antichrist, will be resurrected and will reign with Jesus for the full duration of the Millennial Kingdom. They trusted in Jesus even to the point of death, believing that they would find eternal life through following His way, and God will honour them because of this.

Revelation 20:4 – 'Then I saw the souls of those who had been beheaded for their witness to Jesus and for the word of God, who had not worshiped the beast or his image, and had not received his mark on their foreheads or on their hands. And they lived and reigned with Christ for a thousand years.'

Martyrs will be resurrected and invited into the Promised Land to dwell and reign in the Millennial Kingdom, but no other person from the dead will rise to join them until after the one thousand years are over. Therefore, the people who will live with Jesus in the holy land during these one thousand years, will be the righteous children of God who are already living on earth (and who have faith in Jesus), as well as the resurrected martyrs.

Those who do not live in righteousness, and reject God's ways, will not be part of the assembly drawn back to Israel. Just as righteousness on its own does not lead to salvation, believing in Christ but lacking obedience to His will, also will not lead to salvation. For even demons believe in Jesus and tremble (James 2:19), but they shall be destroyed in the wrath of God. In Isaiah 5:24, God says concerning those who do not walk in obedience:

"Therefore, as the fire devours the stubble, and the flame consumes the chaff, so their root will be as rottenness, and their blossom will ascend like dust; because they have rejected the law of the Lord of hosts, and despised the word of the Holy One of Israel."

Those who reject God's laws and despise His words will rot in death and be consumed by fire. This is a terrifying warning. Whilst God desires that all may be saved and none should perish (2 Peter 3:9), those who choose to go against His laws of protection ultimately choose a fate of destruction. Disobedience to God's ways creates distance from God and His love. Therefore, without repentance this lifestyle can only lead to eternal death – only the Father's forgiveness can make us right with Him again.

Those that remain disobedient and unrepentant will rot and decay. This is because they have chosen not to grow their roots into the life-giving soil and waters of God's words and statutes, which establish an everlasting foundation for those who trust and obey Him. Because their roots have not been grown in God's soil of love and protection, it is impossible for the unrighteous to flourish. They lack blossom and fruit, remaining as stubble in a field, easily consumed by the fire of God's judgement. People who live in continual disobedience to the God of heaven and earth, despising His wisdom, cannot and will not live in the holy land of Israel with His people. If they choose to walk away from God, God will walk away from them.

The following verse from Ezekiel gives more detail about what will happen to those who have rebelled against God.

Ezekiel 20:38 – "I will purge the rebels from among you, and those who transgress against Me; I will bring them out of the country where they dwell, but they shall not enter the land of Israel. Then you will know that I am the Lord."

This verse surprised me when I first came across it. God tells us that some rebels and transgressors will be gathered out of the nations of the world, just as His true children will be. However, they will be shocked that when the journey is nearly over, God forbids them to enter the land promised to Israel. Whilst God does not tell us exactly who these rebels are, it is possible that these are people who outwardly put on the appearance of loving God, but secretly live in sin, following the desires of their flesh. They will travel with God's children but then be publicly shamed when they are blocked from entering. Then everyone shall know and exalt the power of the Lord, who knows the thoughts and hearts of all. No rebels shall dwell in the holy land – they shall be purged out of sight forevermore.

A similar description can be found in **Isaiah 42:17** :

"They shall be turned back, they shall be greatly ashamed, who trust in carved images, who say to the moulded images, 'You are our gods.'"

Only the children of the promise shall enter the glorious land that is the inheritance of Israel. Those who do not fear the Lord or His commands shall not enter - idolators will be shamed by the true King of kings. But God will welcome His children with loving arms, giving them peace and rest, rescuing them from all trouble.

Isaiah 27:13 – 'they will come, who are about to perish in the land of Assyria, and they who are outcasts in the land of Egypt, and shall worship the Lord in the holy mount at Jerusalem.'

Many of the remnant of God's people are currently perishing in the ungodly nations of the world, treated like outcasts in the countries where they have been scattered. Just as Jesus was hated by the world, so too will His followers be (John 15:18-19) . But God shall restore to them all that was lost, bringing them honour because of His great love for them. Together, they will once again worship their Creator in perfect unity, in the land He has promised them since the days of Abraham. What a day it will be when all God's children arrive together! What joy it will bring.

To conclude, here is another passage from the Psalms, which nicely consolidates the ideas explored in this chapter:

Psalm 15:1-5 – 'Lord, who may abide in Your tabernacle? Who may dwell in Your holy hill? He who walks uprightly, and works righteousness, and speaks the truth in his heart; he who does not backbite with his tongue, nor does evil to his neighbour, nor does he take up a reproach against his friend; in whose eyes a vile person is despised, but he honours those who fear the Lord; he who swears to his own hurt and does not change; he who does not put out his money at usury, nor does he take a bribe against the innocent. He who does these things shall never be moved.'

Chapter 5

How the Messiah Will Call Us

There are a number of different scriptures in the Bible from the Old and New Testaments alike, which describe how God will call back His people, gathering them from the nations where they have been scattered. Jesus describes the events that will take place on the day of His return in Matthew 24:29-31:

"Immediately after the tribulation of those days the sun will be darkened, and the moon will not give its light; the stars will fall from heaven, and the powers of the heavens will be shaken. Then the sign of the Son of Man will appear in heaven, and then all the tribes of the earth will mourn, and they will see the Son of Man coming on the clouds of heaven with power and great glory. And He will send His angels with a great sound of a trumpet, and they will gather together His elect from the four winds, from one end of heaven to the other."

At the end of the trials and tribulations of the end times (which are talked about in more detail in the Book of Revelation), the sun and moon will be darkened, and the stars will fall to earth. These are the signs of the Messiah's coming, which we should be awaiting eagerly. When the nations see that Christ is returning, it is said that the earth will mourn. It will be terrifying for those who have lived their lives in opposition to God, denying His existence and blaspheming the King of all creation. His return will come as a delight to His chosen ones, but even they will tremble at the sight of His holiness and might. In great power and glory, Jesus shall descend to earth in the clouds, and every eye shall see Him at once (Revelation 1:7). Jesus will send forth His angels with a great, majestic trumpet sound, heard by all. Angelic hosts will gather the elect of God from all the ends of the earth. What an awesome vision.

It is beautiful that Jesus describes God's people as 'the elect'. In Greek, the terms 'elect' and 'chosen' are used interchangeably and derive from the Greek word 'eklektos', which was used in scripture to refer to those picked out or chosen by God to obtain salvation through Christ. What a privilege to be chosen by the God of all creation! To be a part of His precious people. And to be gathered by the angels, at the request of Christ who sends them.

No one will be able to miss the coming of Jesus. The signs in creation, the trumpet blasts, and the astounding sight of His arrival as He comes with many crowns on His head, riding on a white horse and followed closely behind by the armies of heaven (Revelation 19). The trumpet blasts will not only be a declaration of Christ's return, but also a call to the children of God, letting them know the time has come to enter the Promised Land.

Isaiah confirms that the trumpet blast will proclaim the day of the return of God's people:

Isaiah 27:12-13 – 'And it shall come to pass in that day that the Lord will thresh, from the channel of the River to the Brook of Egypt; and you will be gathered one by one, O you children of Israel. So it shall be in that day: the great trumpet will be blown; they will come [...] and shall worship the Lord in the holy mount at Jerusalem.'

On the day of His return, Christ will gather His people one by one, handpicking them from the nations. Like a shepherd knows his flock, Jesus knows His sheep individually. He will thresh for them as a harvester threshes to separate grain from the chaff, keeping what is valuable and leaving behind what is worthless. The grain is carried all together to the place where it was destined to be. And as a processor converts grain to flour by cracking and rolling it, then sieving out all impurities, so will God cleanse His children from their impurities, refining them in His fire.

On this day, 'the great trumpet will be blown', and God's chosen ones will return to the 'holy mount at Jerusalem' to worship the Lord. The trumpet call to the Promised Land will be loud and unmissable! All the nations of the earth will hear it. This day will mirror what happened in the book of Joshua, when the Israelites marched around Jericho.

Joshua 6:5 – "It shall come to pass, when they make a long blast with the ram's horn, and when you hear the sound of the trumpet, that all the people shall shout with a great shout; then the wall of the city will fall down flat. And the people shall go up every man straight before him."

Joshua 6:16 – 'And the seventh time it happened, when the priests blew the trumpets, that Joshua said to the people: "Shout, for the Lord has given you the city!"'

At the blast of the ram's horn, the city walls of evil Jericho fell down flat, destroyed by the power of God. Similarly, the evil nations of the world will be destroyed in the wrath of God's fury at the coming of Christ. There will be a great shout from all God's people, in jubilant celebration of Christ's victory. They will shout because God has given them the city! The holy city of Jerusalem shall be returned to the people for whom it was always meant. God's promises to Abraham will be fulfilled. 'And the people shall go up every man straight before him' – every man and woman before their Saviour, worshipping Jesus at the holy hill of Zion. The prophetic insights in these verses are incredible, but could easily be missed in the familiarity of the stories. When reading the scriptures, it is important to constantly keep our eyes and ears open to new and fresh revelations from God.

The call of Christ to His children is described in a different, but incredible way below:

Hosea 11:10-11 – '"They shall walk after the Lord. He will roar like a lion. When He roars, then His sons shall come trembling from the west; They shall come trembling like a bird from Egypt, like a dove from the land of Assyria. And I will let them dwell in their houses," says the Lord.'

What an awesome image! Jesus, the Lion of the tribe of Judah, will roar for the sons of God, and they shall follow Him. He will display His might to all the earth, and in a show of strength, will call His children home. Lion roars are incredibly loud and powerful, their calls vibrating through every surrounding living being. Their sound travels for miles over land, sounding close even from afar. In the presence of the King, all creation will be humbled. Like campers hearing the call of a lion beside their tent at night, so will the unrighteous receive a terrifying shock at His roar, at a time they felt safe and did not expect a visit.

From the nations of the earth, God's children will come trembling before their Creator, in awe of His majestic presence. But in beautiful contrast to their fear and trembling, His chosen ones are described as coming 'like a dove'. Whilst in awe of the majesty of God, they shall also feel a great sense of peace, a kind of peace unknown to the sinful world they have come from. In the presence of their Saviour, His children know they are secure and safe. They shall 'walk after the Lord' their Shepherd, to the green pastures prepared for them, beside the quiet waters of His Spirit. They shall dwell in houses given to them by God, safe and at peace.

Isaiah 5:26 says that:

'He will lift up a banner to the nations from afar, and will whistle to them from the end of the earth; surely they shall come with speed, swiftly.'

Christ will lift up a banner for all to see - a visual sign for His children to follow Him and return to their land. In ancient times, and through scripture, banners represented allegiance to God or a nation, and were often used when leading an army to battle (Jeremiah 51:27). They were also used in celebration to declare victory (Psalm 20:5). This banner shall be a sign to all those who are God's chosen ones, who are allies of King Jesus in the battle against evil, that they are victorious. It will proclaim the start of their joyous celebrations - their King has returned and is waiting for their arrival in Israel.

As well as raising the banner, Christ will whistle to His elect, so that they shall hear Him from across the whole earth. The word 'whistle' here, comes from the Hebrew word 'Sharak', which can also be translated as to 'hiss'. This puzzled me at first, as hissing to His children does not fit in with the loving character of God. However, after more research I found that this word can also be used in the context of blowing a whistle - a shepherd's whistle. At that time in history, each shepherd would have their own unique whistle, sounding different from all others, and being recognised only by their sheep. If different flocks became mixed together, the shepherds would blow their whistles. Hearing this, the sheep would recognise and follow the whistle of their own shepherd, walking to the place where their shepherd guides them. Jesus is our Good Shepherd, and upon His return, He will whistle for His sheep! Wherever they have been scattered across the earth, if they are truly His, they will recognise the sound of His call and follow in His direction. They know that they will find safety and security where their Shepherd is.

Through reading God's word and spending time in His presence, we will grow familiar with His voice, so that we will know when it is He Who calls us. Then we shall come running to our Shepherd, our King.

The hurry of God's children as they travel from their nations to the Promised Land, is emphasised in **Zechariah 2:6-7** :

"Up, up! Flee from the land of the north," says the Lord; "for I have spread you abroad like the four winds of heaven," says the Lord. "Up, Zion! Escape, you who dwell with the daughter of Babylon."

There will be a great rush as God's elect flee from the evil lands where they have been dispersed. They will be rescued from Babylon – the city that represents all evil. God will direct them, encouraging them to come quickly - quickly back to the land of their inheritance. The journey may be long, but soon they will be at rest, at home with Jesus, their everlasting King.

Chapter 6

The Great Exodus

When God calls His children to return to the land of Israel from the nations, there will be great joy and celebration! Their journey will be full of exceeding gladness, as they gather together and head to the Promised Land. This is beautifully described in Isaiah 51:11:

'So the ransomed of the Lord shall return, and come to Zion with singing, with everlasting joy on their heads. They shall obtain joy and gladness; sorrow and sighing shall flee away.'

The joy of God's chosen people will be everlasting and uncontainable. The atmosphere will be filled with celebration and singing! What a journey! What a pilgrimage! They will 'obtain' gladness from God and it shall be visible to all, radiating from their faces. Sorrow and sighing, once common when they were dwelling in evil nations, will vanish and be forgotten. In the presence of their King, no one will harm them or cause them trouble. We serve a triumphant God! He is so good to us.

The verse above from Isaiah refers to the children of God as 'the ransomed' ones. This is because Jesus has ransomed us from the curse of sin and death caused by the sin of Adam, paying the price for our freedom with His precious blood on the cross. The Father loved mankind so much, that He paid the price of His son for us. What astounding, boundless love!

We are given more details of the journey in Isaiah 11:16:

'There will be a highway for the remnant of His people who will be left from Assyria, as it was for Israel in the day that he came up from the land of Egypt.'

God will make a clear highway for His people to travel along when journeying back to Israel! It will be miraculous, like the path He created across the Red Sea for the Israelites, when escaping from Egypt with Moses. Waters will part and enemies will be removed from the children of God. Yahweh will make a way where there is no way – those from far nations will not need to use aeroplanes to cross waters, or trains to prevent weariness from travelling. Just as the Israelites left Egypt and followed God's direction to the Promised Land, so will the remnant return, leaving ungodly nations behind them and following the path God has set before them.

Even though this journey may be a long one, it has been promised that God's children shall not grow tired.

Isaiah 5:27-28 – 'No one will be weary or stumble among them, no one will slumber or sleep; nor will the belt on their loins be loosed, nor the strap of their sandals be broken; whose arrows are sharp, and all their bows bent; their horses' hooves will seem like flint, and their wheels like a whirlwind.'

The mention of horses and wheels implies that there will be mass transport by horse and chariot on this great exodus. The horses provided by God for His elect shall have great strength, with hooves like flint, and they shall run with great speed, causing chariot wheels to spin like a whirlwind. God wants His children to hurry away from the evil nations with great speed (Zechariah 2:6-7). They will indeed obey His instruction, and be given supernatural strength to do so. Not one person will grow weary or fall asleep, and all their shoes and clothing will be in good condition. Nothing will prevent their movement forward. They will have sharp arrows to protect themselves against enemies, keeping them safe on their journey to the Promised Land. Another passage in Isaiah proclaims that no wild animals will enter the highway, showing the supernatural protection of God:

Isaiah 35:8-10 – 'A highway shall be there, and a road, and it shall be called the Highway of Holiness. The unclean shall not pass over it, but it shall be for others. Whoever walks the road, although a fool, shall not go astray. No lion shall be there, nor shall any ravenous beast go up on it; it shall not be found there. But the redeemed shall walk there, and the ransomed of the Lord shall return, and come to Zion with singing, with everlasting joy on their heads. They shall obtain joy and gladness, and sorrow and sighing shall flee away.'

Here, the path for the returning remnant of Israel is referred to as the 'Highway of Holiness'. What a glorious title! No unclean, ungodly person will be allowed to walk on it – only those chosen by God to enter His holy city. Although they themselves are only human, and 'fools' without the guidance of God, the elect will never fall astray by following this path. They can be sure they will arrive at the destination of their inheritance. Ravenous beasts will not come upon the Highway of Holiness – God will keep His people safe from the lions just as the prophet Daniel was saved from lions in the den (**Daniel 6**). Nothing can harm the chosen ones, nor will anything stop them from entering the land the Lord has prepared for them.

The last two sentences of this passage sound very similar to **Isaiah 51:11**, as seen earlier. There is such emphasis on the joy and gladness of the people. Truly, this will be the most marvellous journey one could possibly dream of. Imagine leaving behind everything linked with fear, sadness, sin and shame, whilst knowing that the King of all heaven and earth is waiting to receive you at the other side, His banner of love and shepherd's whistle calling you home. Wouldn't you celebrate with all your might? And this is actually going to happen! It is written in the Bible! How incredible!

Here Isaiah refers to God's people as 'redeemed', as well as 'ransomed'. Redeemed, comes from the Hebrew word 'gā'al', which means to buy something back which was lost. God's people had been lost to the nations of the world, but He has called them back to safely live with Him, as in the days of the Garden of Eden. We will forever live in unity with Him, our Saviour and Deliverer.

Not one of God's children will be left out of this promise. The weak shall be made strong in Christ, and He shall guide them.

Isaiah 42:16 – "I will bring the blind by a way they did not know; I will lead them in paths they have not known. I will make darkness light before them, and crooked places straight. These things I will do for them, and not forsake them."

The blind will be led where they have never before dared to travel, now in the safety of their Saviour. What was darkness to them before will now be made light, and they shall see clearly. The Lord will not forsake them – He will not leave even one of His children behind. He is the Good Shepherd - the very best. Every crooked place will be straightened out as a level path for His sheep.

The Shepherd will wonderfully care and provide for His flock.

Isaiah 48:20-21 – 'Go forth from Babylon! Flee from the Chaldeans! With a voice of singing, declare, proclaim this, utter it to the end of the earth; say, "The Lord has redeemed His servant Jacob!" And they did not thirst when He led them through the deserts; He caused the waters to flow from the rock for them; He also split the rock, and the waters gushed out.'

As His elect make the journey to the Promised Land, they may be amazed to see water provided from the rocks as in the time of the great exodus in the days of Moses (**Exodus 17**). Wherever His children are across the nations, their needs will be supplied by their loving Saviour.

As they go on this journey, they shall sing, declare and proclaim to all the lands from where they are fleeing, "the Lord has redeemed His servant Jacob!" All the world will know the Lord's saving power, that He has forgiven the sins of those who put their trust and hope in Him. Surely, those who wait on the Lord will renew their strength, never growing weary or faint, but will soar on wings like eagles (**Isaiah 40:31**). Their joy shall be endless and seen by all!

As well as providing water for them, the Lord will also provide His people with plentiful food. The following verses are prophetic of what is to come:

Psalm 74:14-15 – 'You broke the heads of Leviathan in pieces, and gave him as food to the people inhabiting the wilderness. You broke open the fountain and the flood; You dried up mighty rivers.'

Instead of eating manna in the desert on this future journey back to the promised land, meat will be provided in the form of a creature of biblical proportions. A creature so mighty and powerful that it breathes fire and sneezes light (**Job 41**), will be destroyed effortlessly by the Lord to provide for those He loves. Fountains for drinking will be established, and dried rivers for walking over.

And the Lord Himself will journey with them.

Isaiah 52:12 – 'For you shall not go out with haste, nor go by flight; for the Lord will go before you, and the God of Israel will be your rear guard.'

What a beautiful promise. The God of Israel will be ahead of them as they go, whilst also guarding them from behind – they will be completely encompassed in His presence and protection. No harm will overtake the sons and daughters of the Most High King. The verse also states that the children of God will not leave their nations 'with haste' or 'by flight'. Whilst, at first, this may seem to conflict with the idea of a speedy journey, it can be interpreted as an instruction to the people to leave without fear and anxiety. They do not need to rush in fear of being pursued by enemies because God is protecting them. Their fast speed is solely due to their immense desire to reach the Promised Land, where Jesus shall rule and reign.

Let us meditate on the two following passages to complete our picture of this wonderful journey:

Jeremiah 31:7-9 – 'For thus says the Lord: "Sing with gladness for Jacob, and shout among the chief of the nations; proclaim, give praise, and say, 'O Lord, save Your people, the remnant of Israel!' Behold, I will bring them from the north country, and gather them from the ends of the earth, among them the blind and the lame, the woman with child and the one who labours with child, together; a great throng shall return there. They shall come with weeping, and with supplications I will lead them. I will cause them to walk by the rivers of waters, in a straight way in which they shall not stumble; for I am a Father to Israel, and Ephraim is My firstborn.'"

Isaiah 49:9b-13 – "'They shall feed along the roads, and their pastures shall be on all desolate heights. They shall neither hunger nor thirst, neither heat nor sun shall strike them; for He who has mercy on them will lead them, even by the springs of water He will guide them. I will make each of My mountains a road, and My highways shall be elevated. Surely these shall come from afar; look! Those from the north and the west, and these from the land of Sinim." Sing, O heavens! Be joyful, O earth! And break out in singing, O mountains! For the Lord has comforted His people, and will have mercy on His afflicted.

Chapter 7

Refinement Leads to Holiness

When all the journeying has finished and God's children arrive together in the Promised Land of Israel, God will purify His people. Through a cleansing and refining process, His chosen people will become holy in His sight, set apart for their King. The refining process begun in this life, through trials and suffering, will finally be brought to full completion (1 Peter 1:6-7).

In this passage from Ezekiel, God beautifully describes how He will cleanse the people of Israel with clean water, and give them a new heart:

Ezekiel 36:24-28 – "For I will take you from among the nations, gather you out of all countries, and bring you into your own land. Then I will sprinkle clean water on you, and you shall be clean; I will cleanse you from all your filthiness and from all your idols. I will give you a new heart and put a new spirit within you; I will take the heart of stone out of your flesh and give you a heart of flesh. I will put My Spirit within you and cause you to walk in My statutes, and you will keep My judgments and do them. Then you shall dwell in the land that I gave to your fathers; you shall be My people, and I will be your God."

God will gather His children into the land He promised their ancestors, and there He will set them apart as His people forevermore, putting His Spirit within them. With clean water He will cleanse them completely of their past sins and filthiness. Any idols that they had (things that they had placed at a higher value than God) will be wiped out and no longer remembered. Christ will have no rival in the place where He rules. Their 'heart of stone' which was once governed by earthly desires and sinful thoughts, will be replaced with 'a heart of flesh'. Their new hearts will desire to live only a life that is pleasing to God, without being tempted to fall into sin. God will put His Spirit in His children, giving them the will and the strength to follow all His statutes and judgements without stumbling. With God's Spirit in them, they will become a righteous and holy nation, being obedient to Him in all things. Through their obedience, they will receive God's blessing forevermore, dwelling in the land He promised them from generation to generation. They will be His people, and He will be their God. No one will take them from His hands.

But later on in the passage, God gives them a warning:

Ezekiel 36:31-32 – "Then you will remember your evil ways and your deeds that were not good; and you will loathe yourselves in your own sight, for your iniquities and your abominations. Not for your sake do I do this," says the Lord God, "let it be known to you. Be ashamed and confounded for your own ways, O house of Israel!"

His chosen ones, just like the nations they came from, were an undeserving people who fell short of God's glory by falling into sin – it was not because of their own worthiness that God decided to cleanse them as His holy people. No-one is able to achieve righteousness in their own strength, because they will always fail to live up to God's holy standards. This is exactly why Jesus, the only completely perfect and righteous One, was sent to die for the whole world. Bearing all our sins on the cross, He took our punishment upon Himself, dying the death that we ourselves deserve. Our debt has been paid by the perfect sacrifice of Jesus, Son of God. It is therefore our faith in His death and resurrection that makes us right with the Father - we were never worthy of this love and grace!

No-one can boast of their salvation through works. When God's children become fully cleansed and purified in the land of Israel, it will be as if a veil is removed from their eyes, and they will realise just how terrible their sins have been. They will be very ashamed. But through this revelation, they will come to a greater understanding and awe of the astounding grace of God. Despite all their sin and wrongdoing, God never once stopped loving them, and from the beginning of time He has called them to be His own. He longs to spend eternity with His children, and it is through the sacrifice of Jesus, and this cleansing process, that this will be made possible.

Micah 7:18-20 – 'Who is a God like You, pardoning iniquity and passing over the transgression of the remnant of His heritage? He does not retain His anger forever, because He delights in mercy. He will again have compassion on us, and will subdue our iniquities. You will cast all our sins into the depths of the sea. You will give truth to Jacob and mercy to Abraham, which You have sworn to our fathers from days of old.'

Truly, there is no one like the Lord, and nothing to match the great forgiveness He has for those who repent and put their trust in Him. He will show mercy and compassion to the remnant of His people, and will delight in doing so! His anger is but for a moment, but His favour is for life (Psalm 30:5). It is not because of anything that they have done that God chooses to purify and restore His people, but because of His outrageous unconditional love for them, and for the glory of His name. By His grace, their sins will be cast into the depths of the sea, and the promises given to Abraham, Isaac and Jacob will be fulfilled. He will again make His people a great nation that will be a blessing to the earth, and His children shall dwell in the land of Israel once more.

Isaiah 4:3-4 – 'And it shall come to pass that he who is left in Zion and remains in Jerusalem will be called holy—everyone who is recorded among the living in Jerusalem. When the Lord has washed away the filth of the daughters of Zion, and purged the blood of Jerusalem from her midst, by the spirit of judgment and by the spirit of burning'

When God's children are washed from their old sinful ways, and given a heart of flesh, they will become holy and righteous in God's eyes. What man has failed to do in his own strength, was made possible only through the mercy of God. And what a glorious place Israel will be when all its inhabitants are holy, with not one unclean person dwelling among them. They shall be looked upon as God's people – His precious, chosen ones.

The outcome of this time of cleansing is beautiful. However, the process is not likely to be pain-free. God's refinement will come upon the people as a 'spirit of judgement' and 'burning', ridding them of filthiness. Malachi explains this in more detail:

Malachi 3:2-4 – "But who can endure the day of His coming? And who can stand when He appears? For He is like a refiner's fire and like launderer's soap. He will sit as a refiner and a purifier of silver; He will purify the sons of Levi, and purge them as gold and silver, that they may offer to the Lord an offering in righteousness. Then the offering of Judah and Jerusalem will be pleasant to the Lord, as in the days of old, as in former years."

When Christ returns and draws His people back to Israel, He will be as a refiner's fire to them, purifying His chosen ones. He will craft His people into the most beautiful nation, ridding them of all impurities and making them as pure gold and silver. The Lord their potter will cast off their old sins, perfecting His workmanship, and will cleanse His people with soap, making them white and spotless. It is when God's elect ones enter this new state of holiness, that their offerings and sacrifices will once again become pleasing to Him. What was lost will again be restored, and what was added through sin shall be removed.

Zechariah 13:1-2 – "In that day a fountain shall be opened for the house of David and for the inhabitants of Jerusalem, for sin and for uncleanness. It shall be in that day," says the Lord of hosts, "that I will cut off the names of the idols from the land, and they shall no longer be remembered. I will also cause the prophets and the unclean spirit to depart from the land."

God will plant a fountain in Israel for the cleansing of sins - there will be a constant source of purification, given freely to the people of God. The chosen will forever remain pure and spotless before their King. Never again will they defile themselves with idols, and never again will they be troubled with demons. All that is evil will be removed by the mighty hand of God and will not be permitted to re-enter His holy land. No other god but Jesus will receive glory and honour from His people. And no other nation but Israel will be glorified in the way that God promises to exalt them, as we shall discover.

Chapter 8

Restoring Israel - The Glorified Bride of Christ

After being refined, Israel will become the glorious nation that God has always intended them to be, and Christ shall have His pure and spotless bride.

Isaiah 52:1 – 'Awake, awake! Put on your strength, O Zion; put on your beautiful garments; O Jerusalem, the holy city!'

Zion shall be called to awaken, strengthen and make herself beautiful. Her mourning will be replaced with joy and dancing. Just as in the past, when God dressed Israel in 'fine linen' and 'costly garments', adorning her with jewellery (Ezekiel 16), she shall become a beautiful and glorious queen. Jerusalem will be a holy and wonderful city, its people set apart completely for God.

Ezekiel 36:33-38 – 'Thus says the Lord God: "On the day that I cleanse you from all your iniquities, I will also enable you to dwell in the cities, and the ruins shall be rebuilt. The desolate land shall be tilled instead of lying desolate in the sight of all who pass by. So they will say, 'This land that was desolate has become like the garden of Eden; and the wasted, desolate, and ruined cities are now fortified and inhabited.' Then the nations which are left all around you shall know that I, the Lord, have rebuilt the ruined places and planted what was desolate. I, the Lord, have spoken it, and I will do it." 'Thus says the Lord God: "I will also let the house of Israel inquire of Me to do this for them: I will increase their men like a flock. Like a flock offered as holy sacrifices, like the flock at Jerusalem on its feast days, so shall the ruined cities be filled with flocks of men. Then they shall know that I am the Lord."'

God will rebuild Jerusalem and its surrounding cities, turning them from ruins into mighty fortresses, giving strength and security to His people. After their long journey from afar, they will be given new homes in the country that Christ Himself will rule. The once desolate places will become full of many people, as God increases His sons and daughters like a flock. There will be as many people inhabiting these holy cities as animals present in Jerusalem on a feast day! Thousands of children of God will be together in unity, living harmoniously with one another. What an incredible picture! Surely, since the days that God first promised Abraham the land, this is what He had in mind for His people.

The land will once again be tilled for growing crops, becoming a fertile country for God's chosen ones, and producing food in abundance. Famine and drought will no longer occur. The land will become like the garden of Eden in its beauty and fertility, enjoyed by both man and God. Just as the Lord raised dry bones to life in Ezekiel 37 , so will He restore life to Israel in these days, turning what was once ruined and desolate, into a paradise for His people.

When such a miracle as this occurs, all shall recognise that Yahweh is Lord, and both Israel and the surrounding nations will bring Him honour and praise. He will restore Israel to strength because of His great love for His chosen ones, fulfilling His promises to Abraham, and allowing His name to be glorified over all the earth.

The beginning of Isaiah 62 shows us the delight God takes in His children, and how much He desires to give them His glory!

Isaiah 62:1-5 – 'For Zion's sake I will not hold My peace, and for Jerusalem's sake I will not rest, until her righteousness goes forth as brightness, and her salvation as a lamp that burns. The Gentiles shall see your righteousness, and all kings your glory. You shall be called by a new name, which the mouth of the Lord will name. You shall also be a crown of glory in the hand of the Lord, and a royal diadem in the hand of your God. You shall no longer be termed Forsaken, nor shall your land any more be termed Desolate; but you shall be called Hephzibah, and your land Beulah; for the Lord delights in you, and your land shall be married. For as a young man marries a virgin, so shall your sons marry you; and as the bridegroom rejoices over the bride, so shall your God rejoice over you.'

Isaiah 62:12 – 'And they shall call them The Holy People, The Redeemed of the Lord; And you shall be called Sought Out, A City Not Forsaken.'

For the sake of His people, God will continue working to restore Israel until they become as bright as a burning lamp. They will shine forth in righteousness, just like their Creator. All the people of the earth, including its kings, shall see her glory and be in awe. They will call Israel 'The Holy People, The Redeemed of the Lord' and 'Sought Out, A City Not Forsaken'. What titles!! All the earth shall know that God has redeemed His chosen ones and set them apart as His royal priesthood, a holy nation, a people for His own possession (1 Peter 2:9). God did not forsake them or forget His promise to Abraham – the restoration of Israel shall be completed in His own perfect timing. And worth the wait it will be!

No longer will God's people be known as 'Forsaken' and 'Desolate', but as 'Hephzibah' and 'Beulah'. Hephzibah literally translates to 'my delight is in her', and Beulah is a term for being 'a bride' or 'married'. Israel shall be the bride of Christ and He will take great delight in her! She will be married to Jesus, and no other nation will distract her from Him. Christ will be the rejoicing Bridegroom on the day that He cleanses and glorifies His bride. He will also reveal to her a new and special name from His lips, which until then, has not been known. He will gaze at her lovingly, joyful at the thought of reigning with her for one thousand years.

His people shall become as a crown of glory to the Lord, and a royal diadem in His hand. This is the Creator of all heaven and earth speaking! We are truly His most treasured possession, yet we did nothing to deserve this kind of love and admiration. It is purely through our love of Christ and our faith in Him, that we are cleansed and made righteous. By calling Israel a royal diadem, He is calling her His beautiful queen, one of great royalty and fame. She shall be to Him a crown of glory, one in whom He takes great delight. Oh to be the delight of our Saviour and King! Oh to be a people of glory and beauty before Him!

Zephaniah 3:14-20 – 'Sing, O daughter of Zion! Shout, O Israel! Be glad and rejoice with all your heart, O daughter of Jerusalem! The Lord has taken away your judgments, He has cast out your enemy. The King of Israel, the Lord, is in your midst; you shall see disaster no more. In that day it shall be said to Jerusalem: "Do not fear; Zion, let not your hands be weak. The Lord your God in your midst, the Mighty One, will save; He will rejoice over you with gladness, He will quiet you with His love, He will rejoice over you with singing. I will gather those who sorrow over the appointed assembly, who are among you, to whom its reproach is a burden. Behold, at that time I will deal with all who afflict you; I will save the lame, and gather those who were driven out; I will appoint them for praise and fame in every land where they were put to shame. At that time I will bring you back, even at the time I gather you; for I will give you fame and praise

among all the peoples of the earth, when I return your captives before
your eyes," says the Lord.'

Let us sing, shout and rejoice with all our hearts! With
gladness let us meditate on these promises which God will soon
fulfil! All our sins will be taken from us, and no longer shall we be
weak or afraid. The Lord our King will dwell in the midst of Israel
for one thousand years and forevermore, delivering her from
disaster and trouble. The Mighty One will save, restore, and uplift
His people, taking great delight in them. He will rejoice over His
bride with gladness! He will quiet her with His marvellous love!
All her worries and sadness will be silenced forever in the safety
of His love. With gentleness He shall calm His lover. And He will
rejoice over her with singing! Jesus will sing to Israel, and their joy
will be great. Oh to hear the Saviour singing to His bride. What a
time! What a hope to look forward to!

He will restore all that was lost to His people and give
abundantly more - more than can be imagined or asked for. The
lame, sorrowful and exiled will be appointed for praise and fame
in the very lands where they were once put to shame. They will
be appointed, not only to bring praise and fame to God, but also
to receive praise and fame for themselves. The people who once
despised them will honour them. Surely, the Lord will prepare a
table for those who love Him in the presence of their enemies,
overflowing their cups with goodness and love (**Psalm 23**).

Honour will be given to the humble, just as it was taken from
proud and evil Haman and given by God to Mordecai (**Esther
6**). This humble, God-fearing Jew, was paraded around the city
of Persia on the king's horse, wearing a royal robe and royal crest,
as a reward for helping King Xerxes. Haman, who had previously
plotted to kill Mordecai, and who hated the Jews, was the one
made to parade Mordecai around the city whilst proclaiming to

the Persians, "This is what is done for the man the king delights to honour!" In the same way, Christ our King will exalt those who have given their all to Him, causing them to be praised by those who once afflicted them. It is a great and glorious picture of what is to come.

Isaiah 61:9 – "Their descendants shall be known among the Gentiles, and their offspring among the people. All who see them shall acknowledge them, that they are the posterity whom the Lord has blessed."

God's children and all their descendants will be known among the nations, receiving honour and fame from all they meet. For all generations, they shall be known as the Lord's blessed ones. How amazing! They are the Lord's and forever will be.

Malachi 3:16-18 – 'Then those who feared the Lord spoke to one another, and the Lord listened and heard them; so a book of remembrance was written before Him for those who fear the Lord and who meditate on His name. "They shall be Mine," says the Lord of hosts, "On the day that I make them My jewels. And I will spare them as a man spares his own son who serves him." Then you shall again discern between the righteous and the wicked, between one who serves God and one who does not serve Him.'

This passage reminds us that it is those who fear the Lord and meditate on His name, who shall be raised up and honoured. There is even a book of remembrance dedicated to these people! And God desires to make them His jewels! He treasures them above all else. As a loving father would spare his obedient son, so will the Lord spare those who serve Him. When we choose to fear and honour God, we are adopted into the family of Christ, and receive full sonship of the Father, having the privileges of a true child of God. God will do anything to preserve His children, because they are so precious in His sight. He desires so much for us to live in eternity with Him, that He even sacrificed Jesus, His only heavenly Son, that we might be saved through His death and resurrection. All glory to God in the highest!

Once all the sons and daughters of God are gathered in Israel, He will strengthen and glorify them as His beautiful jewels.

Isaiah 4:2 – 'In that day the Branch of the Lord shall be beautiful and glorious; and the fruit of the earth shall be excellent and appealing for those of Israel who have escaped.'

Every inhabitant of Israel - now a holy people who love and fear God - will make up the Branch of the Lord. They will blossom and grow into full flower, prospering in all that they do. Surrounding nations will see her beauty and know that the Lord is with Israel once again. He is the vine that has given them this abundant life. In this land flowing with milk and honey (Exodus 3:8), the fruit of the earth shall be excellent and appealing - attractive to all who see it. God has blessed His loved ones abundantly.

The Lord's children have settled in the land promised to them, a land of plenty, a land where their Bridegroom, Christ, will dwell and reign forevermore.

Let's conclude by reading and thinking about the following:

Isaiah 61:4-7 – 'And they shall rebuild the old ruins, they shall raise up the former desolations, and they shall repair the ruined cities, the desolations of many generations. Strangers shall stand and feed your flocks, and the sons of the foreigner shall be your ploughmen and your vinedressers. But you shall be named the priests of the Lord, they shall call you the servants of our God. You shall eat the riches of the Gentiles, and in their glory you shall boast. Instead of your shame you shall have double honour, and instead of confusion they shall rejoice in their portion. Therefore in their land they shall possess double; everlasting joy shall be theirs.'

Chapter 9

Restoring Israel – Joy in Abundance

As well as rebuilding and exalting Israel (His bride) as a whole, the Lord will restore the souls of His individual people to fullness of strength and joy. The sheep of His flock will be filled with a great, everlasting happiness, and all sadness will be forgotten.

Jeremiah 31:3-4 – 'The Lord has appeared of old to me, saying: "Yes, I have loved you with an everlasting love; therefore with lovingkindness I have drawn you. Again I will build you, and you shall be rebuilt, O virgin of Israel! You shall again be adorned with your tambourines, and shall go forth in the dances of those who rejoice."'

Because of God's everlasting love and kindness, He will draw His children back to the Promised Land, building up their cities with might and power. In the presence of King Jesus, they will be unable to contain their thanksgiving. Israel will make a triumphant sound to the Lord with tambourines, and shall praise Him with dancing! They shall rejoice like never before, and God will take great pleasure in their worship. True worship comes from a place of delighting in the Lord with our whole beings. Songs of celebration will be heard throughout the land in response to the One who gave them everything.

Isaiah 61 opens with a prophetic passage detailing the purpose of Jesus' life on earth. Some of it will be fulfilled at the time of His return. He will come:

Isaiah 61:32-3 – "To proclaim the acceptable year of the Lord, and the day of vengeance of our God; to comfort all who mourn, to console those who mourn in Zion, to give them beauty for ashes, the oil of joy for mourning, the garment of praise for the spirit of heaviness; that they may be called trees of righteousness, the planting of the Lord, that He may be glorified."

When God plants His children in Israel, they will spring up as trees of righteousness, rooted firmly in Christ their Saviour. He will take vengeance on their enemies, and comfort those who mourn. Their brokenness will be healed in His perfect, transformational love. Heaviness, mourning and ashes will crumble in the presence of our holy, loving and powerful God – there will be no room for sadness in His kingdom. Instead, His bride will be adorned with the oil of joy and garment of praise, creating the most beautiful nation that ever existed. Their joy and praise will complete this beauty. It is in their beauty and righteousness that God will be glorified, and that His name might be known across all the earth, for the marvellous love and grace He has lavished on His chosen ones.

Jeremiah 31:10-14 – "Hear the word of the Lord, O nations, and declare it in the isles afar off, and say, 'He who scattered Israel will gather him, and keep him as a shepherd does his flock.' For the Lord has redeemed Jacob, and ransomed him from the hand of one stronger than he. Therefore they shall come and sing in the height of Zion, streaming to the goodness of the Lord—for wheat and new wine and oil, for the young of the flock and the herd; their souls shall be like a well-watered garden, and they shall sorrow no more at all.

Then shall the virgin rejoice in the dance, and the young men and the old, together; for I will turn their mourning to joy, will comfort them, and make them rejoice rather than sorrow. I will satiate the soul of the priests with abundance, and My people shall be satisfied with My goodness, says the Lord."

The Lord will gather His children to the Promised Land as a wise, gentle shepherd gathers his flock. He will show them great kindness and care as He brings them back from the nations. Through the sacrifice of Christ, God's children have been ransomed and redeemed from their old sinful nature and from the power of the devil who once bound them. Now they are free! They will run to the goodness of their Saviour like a rippling stream, singing His praises on the heights of Zion, God's holy hill.

All ages will rejoice - the young virgins and elderly - dancing together in joyful celebration! People from every class, race and gender will come before Christ as one body of worshippers, as royal priests before His throne. Strength will be given to the weak and old so that they may join in the joyful throng. And sorrow will be no more! There will be nothing in the Millennial Kingdom that could lead to fear or sadness – it will be a place of perfect peace, joy and love.

The souls of God's people 'shall be like a well-watered garden'! Jesus, the Water of Life, will be in the midst of His people for one thousand years and forever, quenching their thirst with His presence. His priests will be satiated with the beauty of His glory and splendour. Because of His hand of comfort, they will be joyful and rejoice. As a well-watered garden, Israel will grow to its full potential, becoming fruitful, abundant and pleasing to behold. The roots of the elect will grow deep into Christ as He reigns over them, satisfying them with His great goodness.

Isaiah 51:3 – 'For the Lord will comfort Zion, He will comfort all her waste places; He will make her wilderness like Eden, and her desert like the garden of the Lord; joy and gladness will be found in it, thanksgiving and the voice of melody.'

His comforting presence will water the land of Zion so that it will become as Eden - full of life, colour and abundance. What was once wilderness and desert land will revive to become a glorious garden for the Lord. Israel will be the place Christ delights in and chooses to make His dwelling place. The people will be full of joy and gladness, singing a beautiful melody of thanksgiving, both day and night.

One can only imagine that this is what life was like for Adam and Eve before the fall. No sin or corruption, just beauty and praise to their Maker, an everlasting session of worship in His presence. Our souls thirst for this today, because it is the original dwelling place where we were created to be. To be filled with joy in the presence of our Maker is our natural habitat. When we enter into that perfect unity with the Lord once again, in the holy city of Jerusalem, we will be filled with overflowing joy and delight - delight that was made possible through the redeeming grace of Jesus Christ.

And this joy will be everlasting.

Isaiah 60:15 – "Whereas you have been forsaken and hated, so that no one went through you, I will make you an eternal excellence, a joy of many generations."

Israel, once a hated and forsaken nation because of the curse of its sins, will be restored and exalted by the Lord because of His mercy and compassion towards the remnant. They will be excellent in His sight and their joy will continue from generation to generation. They themselves will be full of joy, and it will overflow to surrounding nations, so that all the earth will delight themselves in the Lord forevermore.

Chapter 10

Restoring Israel - Overcoming Enemies

In the process of restoring Israel, God will defend His people with great strength and might, defeating their enemies. The wicked will be destroyed, paving the way for His righteous Millennial reign to be established.

Zechariah 2:8-9 – 'For thus says the Lord of hosts: "He sent Me after glory, to the nations which plunder you; for he who touches you touches the apple of His eye. For surely I will shake My hand against them, and they shall become spoil for their servants. Then you will know that the Lord of hosts has sent Me."'

After the glory of Christ's return, and the gathering of His children to Israel, Jesus will shake His hand against the enemies of His holy ones. For these elect ones are the 'apple of His eye', and nothing formed against them will prosper. To be against Christ's beloved bride is to wish destruction upon yourself, for He is highly protective of His glorious people. In the knowledge that they are the apple of His eye, Israel will feel completely safe and secure in Him, trusting their Shepherd to ward off wild animals that may come to attack. Evil nations will be defeated, and all the spoils will be rewarded to the children of God, making them exceedingly great and prosperous.

Zechariah 9:14-17 – 'Then the Lord will be seen over them, and His arrow will go forth like lightning. The Lord God will blow the trumpet, and go with whirlwinds from the south. The Lord of hosts will defend them; They shall devour and subdue with slingstones. They shall drink and roar as if with wine; They shall be filled with blood like basins, like the corners of the altar. The Lord their God will save them in that day, as the flock of His people. For they shall be like the jewels of a crown, lifted like a banner over His land-- for how great is its goodness and how great its beauty! Grain shall make the young men thrive, and new wine the young women.'

The people of Israel will be like beautiful jewels and like a vibrant banner in the hand of their Messiah. Christ will protect His treasured possession with fierceness towards all who are against them, saving them from trouble. He will 'devour and pursue' all unrighteousness so that only the upright remain on earth. Using arrows like lightning and terrifying whirlwinds as His fierce battle techniques, the victory will be His forever. For who can stop the Lord Almighty? It will be an awesome sight in these days. God laughs at His adversaries today, for He knows that their day is coming (**Psalm 37:13**). And it's coming soon.

Micah 4:13 – "Arise and thresh, O daughter of Zion; for I will make your horn iron, and I will make your hooves bronze; you shall beat in pieces many peoples; I will consecrate their gain to the Lord, and their substance to the Lord of the whole earth."

This verse reveals that Israel herself will be called to join Christ in His destruction of the wicked. He will strengthen them, making them powerful warriors with horns of iron and hooves of bronze to thresh out the chaff of the world. What a privilege to join the Messiah in bringing the whole earth under the feet of our conquering King! When war is over, the spoils will be consecrated to the Lord as an offering, to give thanks for all He has done for them. The Lord of the whole earth will be glorified and praised.

Isaiah describes Israel fighting in battle alongside the Lord like a roaring lion:

Isaiah 5:29 – 'Their roaring will be like a lion, they will roar like young lions; yes, they will roar and lay hold of the prey; they will carry it away safely, and no one will deliver.'

The Lord will fill Israel with such strength and boldness that they will become like roaring lions. Just as Jesus, the Lion of the tribe of Judah, roared to them when calling them home, they too will roar to declare their victory and power in Christ. No matter their age, they shall be like young lions filled with the strength of youth. Israel will lay hold of their prey – those who had afflicted them and disobeyed the Lord – and carry them away with ease. No one will be able to deliver those who had turned their backs on God.

The establishment of Christ's rule over the wicked is also mentioned briefly by Paul, in His letter to the Corinthians.

1 Corinthians 15:24-26 – 'Then comes the end, when He delivers the kingdom to God the Father, when He puts an end to all rule and all authority and power. For He must reign till He has put all enemies under His feet. The last enemy that will be destroyed is death.'

Jesus will take all power and authority from the evil kings of this world, and give positions of power instead to His own royal priesthood. During the one thousand years of Christ's reign, all the enemies of God will be put under His feet. When the Millennial Kingdom comes to an end, Christ's kingdom will be given to God the Father, and soon judgement day will begin. The last enemy, death/Satan, will be cast into the lake of fire and brimstone and remain there forever.

Whilst the enemies of Israel are being conquered, goods and spoils of war will flood into Jerusalem, blessing God's holy nation.

Isaiah 60:5 – "Then you shall see and become radiant, and your heart shall swell with joy; because the abundance of the sea shall be turned to you, the wealth of the Gentiles shall come to you."

Israel will become radiant and joyful as they receive the goods of the nations. They will be blessed in abundance through the same people who once afflicted them! As the wealth of the Gentiles come into the Promised Land from every direction, the people shall delight with joy in the Lord their God. He has made them a glorious nation, rescuing and restoring them, as promised to Abraham, Isaac and Jacob. Israel will prosper in all that they do, and the joy of the Lord will forever be in their hearts. Nothing can stand against God's royal priesthood, His holy nation, the people for His own possession.

Chapter 11

The Earth Will Be Full of the Knowledge of God's Glory

When the Messiah returns to earth and establishes His rule, every man will fear and honour Him. He will be glorified before all the nations of the earth, and everyone will worship Him. Not only will the bride be beautiful, but so will the Bridegroom, with eyes like fire and hair as white as wool!

Psalm 50:2 – 'Out of Zion, the perfection of beauty, God will shine forth.'

Zion will be perfectly beautiful and glorious in these days, because of the restoration God brought it through. From this holy hill 'God will shine forth', brighter than the sun and radiant in beauty and light. Here His Kingdom will be established for one thousand years, before this world fades away and a new earth is created. Christ will be great among the nations, and a treasure to the remnant of Israel.

Isaiah 28:5 – 'In that day the Lord Almighty will be a glorious crown, a beautiful wreath for the remnant of his people.'

Christ will be the everlasting reward for His people, the prize awaiting them at the end of their race. He will be a glorious crown of righteousness, as spoken about by Paul in 2 Timothy 4:7-8. Truly, Christ is the most magnificent reward that mankind could ever receive! Our Creator, Saviour, and Redeemer will dwell with us forever, crowning the land with His glory and light. This is the hope that we hold on to! Jesus will be excellent to all who see Him and 'a beautiful wreath' for His remnant. All will see Him and marvel in wonder and awe.

Psalm 48:1-3 – 'Great is the Lord, and greatly to be praised in the city of our God, in His holy mountain. Beautiful in elevation, the joy of the whole earth, is Mount Zion on the sides of the north, the city of the great King. God is in her palaces; he is known as her refuge.'

The place where Christ resides will be 'the joy of the whole earth'! It will be a blessing to all peoples, as promised to Abraham by God in Genesis 12:3: 'in you all the families of the earth shall be blessed'. Israel will be a blessing because of the presence of God in her midst. Christ will dwell in her palaces, in her holy temple. He will be her place of refuge. And the Lord will be praised because of His greatness.

Micah 5:4 – 'And He shall stand and feed His flock in the strength of the Lord, in the majesty of the name of the Lord His God; and they shall abide, for now He shall be great to the ends of the earth'

Even the ends of the earth will know how great our God is. There will be no one in this world who does not tremble at the might of God, our Creator. With strength, Christ will shepherd Israel, His flock. In majesty, He will rule His Kingdom in the name of Yahweh, the Lord. His sheep shall abide securely and at peace, not troubled by predators, disease or lack. Their every need will be provided for, and they will lie down beside living waters of life. The Good Shepherd will be known and honoured by all.

Zephaniah 2:11 – 'The Lord will be awesome to them, For He will reduce to nothing all the gods of the earth; people shall worship Him, each one from his place, indeed all the shores of the nations.'

All wickedness and idols will be destroyed in an instant. Yahweh will be the only God to be worshipped. And He shall receive praise from every nation and every tongue. All places of the earth will be filled with people in worship to the Lord most high! How spectacular! Creation will bow down in awe of their Creator. God will show His awesomeness to all people – no longer will a veil be placed over their eyes, but they will see God face to face in all His marvellous glory (**1 Corinthians 13:12**).

Habakkuk 2:14 – "For the earth will be filled with the knowledge of the glory of the Lord, As the waters cover the sea."

Hallelujah! Every single person on earth will know the glorious wonders of the Lord our God, our Rock and Salvation. This beautiful knowledge will be as abundant as the water in our oceans! Our land will be flooded with the revelation of God's glory and greatness. The deception of the enemy will be banished for one thousand years, and people will see the light of God with new clarity. Men will be ashamed of their wicked ways and come bowing down before God in worship.

Philippians 2:9-11 – 'Therefore God also has highly exalted Him and given Him the name which is above every name, that at the name of

Jesus every knee should bow, of those in heaven, and of those on earth, and of those under the earth, and that every tongue should confess that Jesus Christ is Lord, to the glory of God the Father.'

Isaiah 45:23b – "That to Me every knee shall bow, every tongue shall take an oath."

The Father has exalted Christ, giving Him the name above all names - Yeshua. All those in heaven and on earth will one day bow before our glorious King, confessing that He alone is Lord of all – they will submit completely to their Saviour, trembling at His feet. We are Christ's servants and priests, and we will surrender all to Him for the purpose of His glory. When in the presence of His absolute holiness, we will realise that we truly are a people of unclean lips, in need of purification from Jesus, our High Priest.

Malachi 1:11 – "'For from the rising of the sun, even to its going down, My name shall be great among the Gentiles; in every place incense shall be offered to My name, and a pure offering; for My name shall be great among the nations," Says the Lord of hosts.'

His name will become great among the nations! The Gentiles that once did not know His glory will see it with perfect clarity. Offerings of sacrifice will be made to the Lord from all across the earth and from every tribe and tongue! All earth will be in unity, offering their praises to the King of all kings and Lord of all lords, their worship rising like incense. Altar sacrifices will be made, as we shall explore later, and these shall be perfectly pure - pleasing and acceptable to God. It will be as a return to the days of Israel in the Old Testament, but more glorious.

Zechariah 14:9 – 'And the Lord shall be King over all the earth. In that day it shall be—"The Lord is one," and His name one.'

Whilst the land of Israel will be a place only for the remnant of the Lord's people, His precious possession, Jesus will also rule beyond these borders and to the very ends of the earth. There will be no land and no person that does not come under the reign of the Messiah. His Kingdom will be over all mankind, and Satan will be restrained from deceiving people and leading them away from Christ's marvellous truth. The Lord is one, and there is no one like Him, nor anyone else besides Him.

Isaiah 42:21 – 'The Lord is well pleased for His righteousness' sake; He will exalt the law and make it honourable.'

In His Kingdom, God will make His law glorious and honoured among nations. He created His law to be this way from the start, but many people have since fallen astray, lacking the love and fear of His words and judgements. When Christ reigns on earth, we will wholeheartedly seek to follow His ways, loving righteousness and truth. We will despise what He despises, and delight in what brings Him joy. It is (and has always been) righteousness that pleases God greatly, and sin that brings Him sorrow. For sin comes from the evil one who seeks to steal, to kill and to destroy (John 10:10). But the Lord's commands bring us life, and life to the full. All will see that this is true!

Isaiah 61:11 – 'For as the earth brings forth its bud, as the garden causes the things that are sown in it to spring forth, so the Lord God will cause righteousness and praise to spring forth before all the nations.'

As beautiful flowers blossom and as plants spring up to life in a garden, so will righteousness and praise flood the earth, making it as the paradise of Eden. Seeds of righteousness planted by the word of God, and by His children on earth, will flourish and prosper. All nations will praise the Lord for His goodness and upright ways!

Isaiah 51:4-5 – "Listen to Me, My people; and give ear to Me, O My nation: for law will proceed from Me, and I will make My justice rest as a light of the peoples. My righteousness is near, my salvation has gone forth, and My arms will judge the peoples; the coastlands will wait upon Me, and on My arm they will trust."

God's people, Israel, will listen to the Lord and wait on Him. They will know that obedience to His commands brings blessing, and so His laws should be honoured, meditated upon, and obeyed. On His arm they will trust, as He guides them like a shepherd through life. Christ's justice will be as a light to His people, and His judgements will be perfect. Israel will delight in the ways of the Lord, and serve Him with one accord, fearing His name above all else.

Zephaniah 3:9-13 – "For then I will restore to the peoples a pure language, that they all may call on the name of the Lord, to serve Him with one accord. From beyond the rivers of Ethiopia My worshipers, the daughter of My dispersed ones, shall bring My offering. In that day you shall not be shamed for any of your deeds in which you transgress against Me; for then I will take away from your midst those who rejoice in your pride, and you shall no longer be haughty In My holy mountain. I will leave in your midst a meek and humble people, and they shall trust in the name of the Lord. The remnant of Israel shall do no unrighteousness and speak no lies, nor shall a deceitful tongue be found in their mouth; for they shall feed their flocks and lie down, and no one shall make them afraid."

Israel will be given a pure, single language, so that all people will understand one another, regardless of what nations they have been drawn from. Together they will call out to God, and desire to serve Him continually. We shall be His worshippers, bringing offerings that are pleasing to Him. Truly, Christ deserves all the praise that we can bring Him!

He will cleanse us from the shame of our sins and purify our hearts so that we will become a meek and humble people, servants of the Most High King. Any feelings of arrogance and superiority will disappear, as we realise our humble position before our Saviour. Pride, the very sin through which Satan fell, will be forever abolished from Christ's holy nation, preventing any of His chosen ones falling into the same fate. Jesus Himself taught us that 'Whoever exalts himself will be humbled, and he who humbles himself will be exalted' (Matthew 23:12). We will be humbled so that Christ can exalt us among the nations!

No one will make Israel afraid. They will be the righteous children of God, protected by His laws and receiving great blessings as they joyfully walk in His statutes.

Jeremiah 31:31-34 – "Behold, the days are coming, says the Lord, when I will make a new covenant with the house of Israel and with the house of Judah— not according to the covenant that I made with their fathers in the day that I took them by the hand to lead them out of the land of Egypt, My covenant which they broke, though I was a husband to them, says the Lord. But this is the covenant that I will make with the house of Israel after those days, says the Lord: I will put My law in their minds, and write it on their hearts; and I will be their God, and they shall be My people. No more shall every man teach his neighbour, and every man his brother, saying, 'Know the Lord,' for they all shall know Me, from the least of them to the greatest of them, says the Lord. For I will forgive their iniquity, and their sin I will remember no more."

In many ways we can interpret the renewed covenant commencing when Christ came to earth 2000 years ago, but it will only reach its complete fulfilment in the Millennial Kingdom. Old things will be made new, and what was once broken will be restored. The old covenant promise made to Israel was broken when the people chose to turn away from God, despite the love that He had shown them. But in His loving kindness and mercy, Christ will reconcile the remnant of Israel to His promise, giving them a new and perfect covenant, flawless and rich with blessings. In this new covenant, God's laws will be written on the hearts and minds of His people. Their flesh will desire to obey God's law and not break it. They will not have to memorise the details of God's law – they shall know it instinctively. And it shall bring life to their bones, making them flourish as a beautiful garden. They will be God's people – in complete likeness of Him – walking in His righteous ways, as His holy nation.

Everyone in these days will know God. They won't just recognise His name – they will know the fullness of His character. The whole earth will be full of the knowledge of Yahweh's glory. Hallelujah! And in His great mercy, God will completely forgive the sins of Israel's remnant. He will guide them in His righteous ways, replacing their heart of stone with a heart of flesh. Forever, they will worship their Creator in spirit and in truth, glorifying Christ in all that they do.

Psalm 66:3-4 – 'Say to God, "How awesome are Your works! Through the greatness of Your power Your enemies shall submit themselves to You. All the earth shall worship You and sing praises to You; they shall sing praises to Your name."'

When Christ returns from heaven in triumph and victory, all His enemies will submit to Him in fear, and the whole earth will sing praises to the King of all creation! For the Lord has no rivals, and no one can match His strength and power. Together, everyone on earth will praise Him and glorify Him – Christ will receive the adoration and honour He so rightly deserves. Forever we will sing of His goodness, and worship Him for His holiness. Not just in Israel, but to the very ends of the earth, God shall be glorified.

Chapter 12

The Messiah's Reign in Zion

During the Millennial Kingdom, Jesus will dwell in the midst of His people, reigning over them with righteous power.

Zechariah 2:10-13 – "Sing and rejoice, O daughter of Zion! For behold, I am coming and I will dwell in your midst," says the Lord. "Many nations shall be joined to the Lord in that day, and they shall become My people. And I will dwell in your midst. Then you will know that the Lord of hosts has sent Me to you. And the Lord will take possession of Judah as His inheritance in the Holy Land, and will again choose Jerusalem. Be silent, all flesh, before the Lord, for He is aroused from His holy habitation!"

The Messiah tells us to rejoice, and delight in the knowledge that He is coming back soon! We should rejoice in the hope that our Lord will Shepherd over us in the Promised Land. People from many nations will dwell together with their Messiah, who will be sent to His people by the Lord of Hosts. For we are God's precious possession, and He cares for us deeply. Jerusalem will be chosen as Christ's inheritance, His dwelling place on earth for one thousand years. And all flesh will fall silent before His majesty and splendour, giving Him honour and reverence. For our God is an awesome God.

Zechariah 8:8 – 'I will bring them back, and they shall dwell in the midst of Jerusalem. They shall be My people And I will be their God, In truth and righteousness.'

We shall be His people, and He shall be our God! Nothing can separate us from His love and protection. And nothing will stop us from giving Him our adoration and worship. We will live in perfect harmony with Christ, in a fellowship marked by truth and righteousness. We will walk in His righteous ways, and His perfect truth will be embedded deep within our hearts.

Zechariah 8:3 – "Thus says the Lord: 'I will return to Zion, and dwell in the midst of Jerusalem. Jerusalem shall be called the City of Truth, The Mountain of the Lord of hosts, The Holy Mountain.'"

When Christ returns to Zion, Jerusalem shall be given glorious new titles. God has restored and exalted His people, making them holy like Himself and clean from all impurities. Because of the purity of Israel and the presence of their King, Mount Zion will be called 'The Holy Mountain'. Christ, named 'Faithful and True' (**Revelation 19:11**), will reign from His 'City of Truth'. And all the city's inhabitant will know that Jesus is the Way, the Truth and the Life, and that there is none besides Him. Anything in opposition to His truth is a lie. Christ's dwelling place will be called 'The Mountain of the Lord of hosts'. The whole world will gaze upon His beauty and splendour at the top of Mount Zion and be in awe.

Isaiah 41:8-10 – "But you, Israel, are My servant, Jacob whom I have chosen, the descendants of Abraham My friend. You whom I have taken from the ends of the earth, and called from its farthest regions, and said to you, 'You are My servant, I have chosen you and have not cast you away: Fear not, for I am with you; be not dismayed, for

I am your God. I will strengthen you, yes, I will help you, I will uphold you with My righteous right hand.'"

God's elect have been chosen by God to be His special people, His servants. From the ends of the earth the Lord will gather His chosen ones, grafting them into the family of Abraham, His friend, and making them part of Israel. The Lord will be their God and He will never leave their side – His love for them is unfathomable. Forever, Israel will be strengthened and helped by Christ their Bridegroom. God's righteous right hand will forever uphold and sustain them - no object and no person will harm His people.

Psalm 46:5-6 – 'God is in the midst of her, she shall not be moved; God shall help her, just at the break of dawn. The nations raged, the kingdoms were moved; He uttered His voice, the earth melted.'

Towards the end of age, we are warned in scripture that the nations will rage and the kingdoms of the earth will be moved. However, the Lord is all powerful and will help His chosen ones throughout these trials and tribulations, keeping them from being shaken by surrounding events. For our God is a mighty conqueror! With an uttering of a word, He can melt the whole earth. The wicked dissolve in His holy presence. And for one thousand years, Christ will reign in the midst of Israel, and the whole earth will be under His submission. For He has the power to give life, and to take life. With matchless strength, Israel will have the greatest Protector of all, King Jesus. Forever He will reign.

As well as being Israel's fierce Protector, Christ will also be their Guide, Provider and Healer.

Micah 4:1-7 – 'Now it shall come to pass in the latter days that the mountain of the Lord's house shall be established on the top of the mountains, and shall be exalted above the hills; and peoples shall flow to it. Many nations shall come and say, "Come, and let us go up to the mountain of the Lord, to the house of the God of Jacob; He will teach us His ways, and we shall walk in His paths." For out of Zion the law shall go forth, and the word of the Lord from Jerusalem. He shall judge between many peoples, and rebuke strong nations afar off; they shall beat their swords into ploughshares, and their spears into pruning hooks; nation shall not lift up sword against nation, neither shall they learn war anymore. But everyone shall sit under his vine and under his fig tree, and no one shall make them afraid; for the mouth of the Lord of hosts has spoken. For all people walk each in the name of his god, but we will walk in the name of the Lord our God forever and ever. "In that day," says the Lord, "I will assemble the lame, I will gather the outcast and those whom I have afflicted; I will make the lame a remnant, and the outcast a strong nation; so the Lord will reign over them in Mount Zion From now on, even forever."'

The lame, the outcast and the afflicted will become a strong nation, ruled by the Lord in Israel. The Lord's house – His holy temple – will be established upon Mount Zion, and people from across the nations shall flow to it to worship the King of kings. For Zion will be known among the nations as the Lord's dwelling place, and all people will seek to travel there. His mount shall be exalted higher than surrounding mountains, and from there, Christ shall rule the earth and care for Israel, His holy nation. He will send forth His laws and teach His ways to all. Christ's words will be a light to our path, and everyone in Israel will follow His guidance – not one will disobey. We will honour and respect His words as righteous, holy and perfect. We will meditate on them day and night. Oh to have such a pure and perfect government in charge of the earth!

Christ will also judge the nations, having wisdom even greater than Solomon, solving disputes and troubles among many people. There will no longer be need for war – all conflicts will be solved by King Jesus, our Prince of Peace. Battles will be non-existent for the one thousand years of His rule. And in Israel, the Lord's people shall live in perfect peace with nothing to make them afraid – every one of them shall sit under his own vine and fig tree in quietness and calm. They will walk in the name of their God forever, protected constantly by His might, love and wisdom.

Zechariah 9:10 – "I will cut off the chariot from Ephraim and the horse from Jerusalem; the battle bow shall be cut off. He shall speak peace to the nations; His dominion shall be 'from sea to sea, And from the River to the ends of the earth.'"

We established earlier that upon Christ's second coming, there will be fierce battles against Israel's enemies, to cleanse the earth of evil. However, these battles will not last for long – Christ, our mighty conqueror, can destroy His enemies in the blink of an eye if He chooses to. Once wickedness has been wiped out, war will be learnt no more, as there will no longer be need for battle. (This is with the exception of the final battle against wickedness when the one thousand years are over, in Revelation 20:7-10.) Instead of wickedness and war, there will be a great peace over the land, like such never felt before since the Garden of Eden. This peace will extend to the very ends of the earth, settling wherever Christ's dominion is in place – everywhere! Fear is a lie spoken from the devil, who wants to steal our joy. When the devil is locked up, there will be no one to pervert Christ's spoken words of peace, which will ring true to every living being.

Isaiah 9:6-7 – 'For unto us a Child is born, unto us a Son is given; and the government will be upon His shoulder. And His name will be called Wonderful, Counsellor, Mighty God, Everlasting Father, Prince of Peace. Of the increase of His government and peace there will be no end, upon the throne of David and over His kingdom, to order it and establish it with judgment and justice from that time forward, even forever. The zeal of the Lord of hosts will perform this.'

This passage is a famous prophecy about Jesus and who He is, spoken around seven hundred years before His birth! Our God is not bound by time or space. Many of the titles given here have not yet been fulfilled, but will be revealed fully on Christ's second coming. Instead of arriving to earth as a humble babe, He will come as Mighty God. Instead of being dismissed and rejected by Israel, He will be called their excellent Counsellor, honoured and respected by all. He is Everlasting, forever dwelling with His people, and will be a Father in His comfort to them. Christ will be their Prince of Peace forever. And the government will be upon His shoulders – all authority shall be His.

Jesus, descendant of David, will establish a government of peace over the earth. The world will be ruled with His righteous judgement and justice, forever. With great zeal and passion, God will send His kingdom to earth, establishing it as in heaven. This is what we have been praying for! For God's kingdom to come and for His will to be done, here on earth as in heaven (**Matthew 6:10**). Whilst for now God's kingdom shines through into our lives and world as a dim reflection, the glory of the full arrival of His Kingdom in the Millenium will shine in all its brilliance. The earth will run in a way that is pleasing to God, and His original design for mankind will be restored – a harmonious life of peace, love, and joy, where we worship and honour Christ and Yahweh.

Isaiah 66:12-13 – 'For thus says the Lord: "Behold, I will extend peace to her like a river, and the glory of the Gentiles like a flowing stream. Then you shall feed; on her sides shall you be carried, and be dandled on her knees. As one whom his mother comforts, so I will comfort you; and you shall be comforted in Jerusalem."'

Jesus was always prophesied to be our great Prince of Peace (Isaiah 9:6), and Emmanuel, God with us (Matthew 1:23). When God resides among us, we will be covered in His perfect peace. Even now, we can feel His peace in our lives through His helper, the Holy Spirit. Yet we shall have a greater measure of it in the Millennial Kingdom, and it shall flow among us like a river, like a flowing stream. This promise has been extended to the Gentiles as well as the Jews – it is for all the children of God who will be gathered in Jerusalem. Here, Christ will care for His people as a mother comforts their child. His affection over His bride knows no bounds. He even took His life for her upon the cross. Israel will be greatly comforted, for after having been through many trials and tribulations, she is now home with her Saviour.

Isaiah 51:16 – "And I have put My words in your mouth; I have covered you with the shadow of My hand, that I may plant the heavens, lay the foundations of the earth, and say to Zion, 'You are My people.'"

God has written His laws on the hearts of His people – His words will constantly be on their lips. They are a people made in His image, who will love what He loves and hate what He hates, reflecting His glory. The Lord covers His nation with the shadow of His hand. They are the apple of His eye, and no harm will come to them. Israel will be completely in His hands, surrounded by His loving care and kindness. For the same God who planted the heavens and laid the earth's foundations calls us His own! This is astounding! The Millennial Kingdom will be one of safety and rest, as the children of God dwell with their Prince of Peace, their Bridegroom.

A beautiful summary of this time is written in the following prophetic Psalm:

Psalm 72:1-17 – 'Give the king Your judgments, O God, and Your righteousness to the king's Son. He will judge Your people with righteousness, and Your poor with justice. The mountains will bring peace to the people, and the little hills, by righteousness. He will bring justice to the poor of the people; He will save the children of the needy, and will break in pieces the oppressor.

They shall fear You as long as the sun and moon endure, throughout all generations. He shall come down like rain upon the grass before mowing, like showers that water the earth. In His days the righteous shall flourish, and abundance of peace, until the moon is no more.

He shall have dominion also from sea to sea, and from the River to the ends of the earth. Those who dwell in the wilderness will bow before Him, and His enemies will lick the dust. The kings of Tarshish and of the isles will bring presents; the kings of Sheba and Seba will offer gifts. Yes, all kings shall fall down before Him; all nations shall serve Him.

For He will deliver the needy when he cries, the poor also, and him who has no helper. He will spare the poor and needy, and will save the souls of the needy. He will redeem their life from oppression and violence; and precious shall be their blood in His sight.

And He shall live; and the gold of Sheba will be given to Him; prayer also will be made for Him continually, and daily He shall be praised.

There will be an abundance of grain in the earth, on the top of the mountains; its fruit shall wave like Lebanon; and those of the city shall flourish like grass of the earth.

His name shall endure forever; His name shall continue as long as the sun. And men shall be blessed in Him; all nations shall call Him blessed.'

Chapter 13

A Kingdom of Prosperity

With Israel restored, and Christ dwelling in her midst, the land, people and animals will prosper greatly. All nations of the earth will see the goodness that the Lord has blessed her with and be amazed.

Jeremiah 33:7-9 – 'And I will cause the captives of Judah and the captives of Israel to return, and will rebuild those places as at the first. I will cleanse them from all their iniquity by which they have sinned against Me, and I will pardon all their iniquities by which they have sinned and by which they have transgressed against Me. Then it shall be to Me a name of joy, a praise, and an honour before all nations of the earth, who shall hear all the good that I do to them; they shall fear and tremble for all the goodness and all the prosperity that I provide for it.'

The cities will be rebuilt, and the people will be cleansed of their sins through the power of God. The Lord will give Israel a name of joy, praise and honour! Forever they will praise and worship God with great pleasure and delight. Surrounding nations will see this and tremble at the uncontainable joy God has given His people. Israel will be blessed with goodness and prosperity, for the Lord delights in His children.

The land shall increase in fertility and the cities shall grow in strength and numbers.

Ezekiel 36:8-12 – "But you, O mountains of Israel, you shall shoot forth your branches and yield your fruit to My people Israel, for they are about to come. For indeed I am for you, and I will turn to you, and you shall be tilled and sown. I will multiply men upon you, all the house of Israel, all of it; and the cities shall be inhabited and the ruins rebuilt. I will multiply upon you man and beast; and they shall increase and bear young; I will make you inhabited as in former times, and do better for you than at your beginnings. Then you shall know that I am the Lord. Yes, I will cause men to walk on you, My people Israel; they shall take possession of you, and you shall be their inheritance; no more shall you bereave them of children."

We will soon be entering the Promised Land, and it shall indeed bear fruit for us! For all creation obeys the commands of God – what He puts His hand to bless, will be blessed. In preparation for our arrival, the land will be tilled and sown, ready for planting and harvesting. The people of Israel will have their every need provided for, and will never hunger or thirst again, under the rule of King Jesus.

The old ruins in Israel will be rebuilt into great cities, inhabited by God's royal priesthood, His chosen ones. Both people and animals will increase greatly in number, producing much offspring. The land will be full of new life. And Israel will become more glorious than at its beginnings - even greater than when Solomon ruled as king, with all His riches and fame, when the Lord's temple was new and beautiful. Even greater than this will Israel be, in the days of the Millennial Kingdom. How amazing! When God's chosen ones receive this marvellous inheritance, all will know that Yahweh is Lord, and that He is determined to do good to Jerusalem.

Zechariah 8:12-15 – 'For the seed shall be prosperous, the vine shall give its fruit, the ground shall give her increase, and the heavens shall give their dew-- I will cause the remnant of this people to possess all these. And it shall come to pass that just as you were a curse among the nations, O house of Judah and house of Israel, so I will save you, and you shall be a blessing. Do not fear, let your hands be strong.' "For thus says the Lord of hosts: 'Just as I determined to punish you when your fathers provoked Me to wrath,' Says the Lord of hosts, 'And I would not relent, so again in these days I am determined to do good to Jerusalem and to the house of Judah. Do not fear.'

All of creation will work together in response to God, to bless His children in the Promised Land. At the Lord's instruction, seed will prosper, vines will grow fruit, land will yield its increase, and dew will be sent down from the heavens. Though the earth may be shaken in the events prior to Christ's coming, it will flourish and revive during His one-thousand-year rule.

Instead of being determined to punish Israel because of their disobedience to Him, God will determine to do good. For His people have been made pure and holy through the blood of Christ, and He has made a new covenant with them, one of righteousness and truth. They shall not be afraid – for God is with them, not against them, and He shall cause their land to prosper and bear much fruit. The Almighty God is intent on blessing them and fulfilling the promises that He made to their forefathers. And Israel shall become a blessing to all those around them, reflecting the light and love of Christ to all nations. Jerusalem will be a praise among the earth.

Isaiah 62:6-9 – 'I have set watchmen on your walls, O Jerusalem; they shall never hold their peace day or night. You who make mention of the Lord, do not keep silent, and give Him no rest till He establishes and till He makes Jerusalem a praise in the earth. The Lord has sworn by His right hand and by the arm of His strength: "Surely I will no longer give your grain as food for your enemies; and the sons of the foreigner shall not drink your new wine, for which you have laboured. But those who have gathered it shall eat it, and praise the Lord; those who have brought it together shall drink it in My holy courts.'"

This passage tells us that we should not stop crying out to God in prayer until He restores His people to the Promised Land and establishes Jerusalem, making them a praise on the earth. Although God has already promised us that these things will take place, He still wants us to ask Him for their fulfilment, and to pray fervently until His promises come to pass. God wants to keep us involved in His plans! We are His servants and royal priesthood, and we should not keep silent. We were born for such a time as this!

When Israel turned away from God in the past, they fell under the curse of disobedience. One of the warnings given in **Deuteronomy 28** was that disobedience to God's commands would make their crops and livestock cursed (**verse 18**). As a result of this, when Israel turned to idol worship and sin, God gave their grain to their enemies, and their wine to foreigners. However, when Christ returns and gathers His people back to the Promised Land, this curse will be broken – His people will be fully redeemed from the bondage of sin and its curses. They will be cleansed of their disobedience because of their repentance and faith in Christ, who has purified their hearts and put His Spirit within them. No longer will the produce of Israel's land go to other nations, but they will eat of it themselves and be glad, praising the Lord. They will drink of it together in God's holy courts! All that was lost in the curse will be restored, and all suffering will be replaced with unending joy.

The Lord's people shall be exalted because they have been made righteous in Christ. Israel will receive the blessings that come with obedience (spoken by Moses in Deuteronomy), because in the Millennial Kingdom, all inhabitants of Israel will follow the ways of the Lord, keeping His statutes.

Deuteronomy 28:8-12 – "The Lord will command the blessing on you in your storehouses and in all to which you set your hand, and He will bless you in the land which the Lord your God is giving you. The Lord will establish you as a holy people to Himself, just as He has sworn to you, if you keep the commandments of the Lord your God and walk in His ways. Then all peoples of the earth shall see that you are called by the name of the Lord, and they shall be afraid of you. And the Lord will grant you plenty of goods, in the fruit of your body, in the increase of your livestock, and in the produce of your ground, in the land of which the Lord swore to your fathers to give you. The Lord will open to you His good treasure, the heavens, to give the rain to your land in its season, and to bless all the work of your hand. You shall lend to many nations, but you shall not borrow."

These verses from Deuteronomy match up perfectly with prophecies from Old Testament prophets relating to what will take place in the Millennial Kingdom! The Lord will command blessing for the God-fearing remnant of His people - both upon their land and upon the works of their hands. He will grant them plenty of goods and will open the heavens, His treasure, pouring out rain in abundance upon their crops. All prosperity and goodness of the land will come from God and God alone. For the Lord delights in blessing His holy people, and all other nations will fear Israel because they are called by His name.

The produce of the land - the land promised to Abraham, Isaac and Jacob - will greatly increase upon the arrival of God's elect. Their flocks and herds will also expand and prosper, as well as their crops.

Isaiah 65:9-10 – "I will bring forth descendants from Jacob, and from Judah an heir of My mountains; My elect shall inherit it, and My servants shall dwell there. Sharon shall be a fold of flocks, and the Valley of Achor a place for herds to lie down, for My people who have sought Me."

From Judah, God's heir will rule – King Jesus! And all His servants will inherit the land of Israel, dwelling in His presence. Because the elect lived their lives seeking God and His kingdom of righteousness, they will receive what they sought for, being encompassed by Christ's peace and provision in the Promised Land. Those who thirst for righteousness shall be filled (Matthew 5:6). The Sharon Plain and Valley of Achor will be given as resting places for the flocks and herds of Israel. Grassland shall be plentiful and productive, and livestock will lack no good thing, just like their owners.

Zephaniah 2:6-7 – 'The seacoast shall be pastures, with shelters for shepherds and folds for flocks. The coast shall be for the remnant of the house of Judah; they shall feed their flocks there; In the houses of Ashkelon they shall lie down at evening. For the Lord their God will intervene for them, and return their captives.'

God cares about every detail of the lives of His people. He will provide the shepherds with shelters along the seacoast, and folds for their flocks. They will not be weary, but will have safe places to lay down and rest. When the shepherds finish feeding their flocks in the evenings, they will be provided with houses to sleep in at night and to lay their heads.

It is interesting to note that in the Millennial Kingdom, farming will continue as before, providing people with their food. Mankind will still have to work the land, but instead of in sweat and toil, with thorns and thistles (**Genesis 3:17-19**), they shall do it in joy and with ease. Farming shall be a blessed occupation, and God will cause the land to yield abundantly, without problems of disease or famine.

Ezekiel 36:29-30 – "I will deliver you from all your uncleannesses. I will call for the grain and multiply it, and bring no famine upon you. And I will multiply the fruit of your trees and the increase of your fields, so that you need never again bear the reproach of famine among the nations."

Famine, which will become more common in the times leading up to Christ's arrival (**Matthew 24:7**), will no longer occur in the land of Israel during these one thousand years. Instead, yields will increase, and the fruit of the trees will be multiplied. Israel will be like the Garden of Eden in its productivity and abundance.

The small, humble remnant of Israel will become an expansive and glorious nation. There is an interesting parable given by God in the book of Ezekiel, comparing the restoration of the Lord's chosen ones, to the growth of a majestic cedar tree:

Ezekiel 17:22-24 – 'Thus says the Lord God: "I will take also one of the highest branches of the high cedar and set it out. I will crop off from the topmost of its young twigs a tender one, and will plant it on a high and prominent mountain. On the mountain height of Israel I will plant it; and it will bring forth boughs, and bear fruit, and be a majestic cedar. Under it will dwell birds of every sort; in the shadow of its branches they will dwell. And all the trees of the field shall know that I, the Lord, have brought down the high tree and exalted the low tree, dried up the green tree and made the dry tree flourish; I, the Lord, have spoken and have done it.'"

In this parable, I believe that the high cedar represents the people of original Israel, who turned from God in disobedience and idolatry. Though they were once exalted and beautiful, established by God, He brought them down and dried them up because of their unfruitfulness. However, a portion of Israel – the remnant that feared God and obeyed His voice (including grafted in Gentiles) – are like the young and tender twig, which will be broken off the cedar, and planted on a high and prominent mountain. This is likely to be the holy hill of Zion. Planted here, God will cause this tender twig to grow into a majestic cedar, which will flourish and bear much fruit. It will prosper under the care and nourishment of the Lord. The tree shall become so full of life, that birds of every sort will dwell in the shadows of its branches, at peace and at rest. And all the trees of the field – all the surrounding nations – will know that this has been the Lord's doing. God will exalt those who love and fear Him, and lower those who turn from Him.

The Lord will be mightily praised for all the blessings He has lavished on His chosen ones. All people will bless Him for His marvellous works, and forever, Christ will be glorified.

Psalm 72:16-19 – 'There will be an abundance of grain in the earth, on the top of the mountains; its fruit shall wave like Lebanon; and those of the city shall flourish like grass of the earth. His name shall endure forever; His name shall continue as long as the sun. And men shall be blessed in Him; all nations shall call Him blessed. Blessed be the Lord God, the God of Israel, who only does wondrous things! And blessed be His glorious name forever! And let the whole earth be filled with His glory. Amen and Amen.'

Chapter 14

Healings and Water of Life

In the Millennial Kingdom, Israel will be a miraculous place, full of life and healings. God's kingdom will be here on earth just as in heaven, and it will be spectacular.

Isaiah 35:5-7 – 'Then the eyes of the blind shall be opened, And the ears of the deaf shall be unstopped. Then the lame shall leap like a deer, and the tongue of the dumb sing. For waters shall burst forth in the wilderness, and streams in the desert. The parched ground shall become a pool, and the thirsty land springs of water; in the habitation of jackals, where each lay, there shall be grass with reeds and rushes.'

The blind will see, the deaf will hear, the lame shall leap and the dumb will sing! Hallelujah! God won't just restore what was lost, but He will go a step further, awakening souls as well as bodies. Not only will the lame and dumb walk and talk, but they will also leap and sing with joy! No disabilities will remain among God's holy people - they will be made perfect in form and in strength. Our God gives life and life to the fullest (John 10:10). All the Lord's people shall praise His name and delight in His wonderful love.

Life and rushing waters will spring forth from barren and empty lands. Places of wilderness, desert, parched ground and thirsty land, will be filled with waters, streams, pools and springs. Dry bones shall come to life (Ezekiel 37) and God's Spirit shall fall on His people like rushing waters. The devil's destructive powers will not touch the earth for one thousand years. With the father of death locked up, life will spring forth in abundance. Vegetation will flourish, providing a soft ground for animals to rest on. All life with thrive in the goodness of God.

There is a specific river in the Millennial Kingdom which flows from the right side of Christ's holy temple. It is seen by Ezekiel in a vision, and is described below:

Ezekiel 47:7-9 – 'When I returned, there, along the bank of the river, were very many trees on one side and the other. Then he said to me: "This water flows toward the eastern region, goes down into the valley, and enters the sea. When it reaches the sea, its waters are healed. And it shall be that every living thing that moves, wherever the rivers go, will live. There will be a very great multitude of fish, because these waters go there; for they will be healed, and everything will live wherever the river goes."'

A river flows from the holy temple, with many trees growing on both its sides. This rushing stream provides plentiful water to the roots of the vegetation around it, just as the Spirit of God gives life to those who dwell in His presence, and to those who establish their roots in His word. The water from this river flows into the valley and then the sea, healing everything in its path and restoring life to every living creature. Oceans are often used in the Bible as a representation of wickedness and sin. Just as the Lords' river enters and heals the sea in this passage, so will the Spirit of God enter the hearts of sinners and restore them to life and righteousness. He will heal His chosen people of all their iniquity, because their souls have thirsted for the Water of Life. Under the reign of Christ, the people will prosper and multiply - there will be a great multitude of fish in the waters of His presence. This passage can also be taken very literally. The river of the Millennial Kingdom will have healing properties, giving abundant life to every living thing that it touches.

Psalm 46, written by the sons of Korah, talks about the same river:

Psalm 46:4 – 'There is a river whose streams shall make glad the city of God, the holy place of the tabernacle of the Most High.'

This river will produce many smaller streams, flowing through the city of God. Its water shall make the people glad, bringing life and joy to the inhabitants of Israel! This verse also tells us that the tabernacle of the Most High will dwell among the people in Jerusalem.

Ezekiel's vision goes on to describe the trees found by the riverbanks:

Ezekiel 47:12 – "Along the bank of the river, on this side and that, will grow all kinds of trees used for food; their leaves will not wither, and their fruit will not fail. They will bear fruit every month, because their water flows from the sanctuary. Their fruit will be for food, and their leaves for medicine."

Along the riverbanks, there will be many kinds of fruit bearing trees. They will be used as food for the inhabitants of Israel. These trees will never wither or die – their source of life will come from the river that flows from the holy temple of Jesus Christ. Every single month they will bear fruit, and they will never become unproductive. Their leaves will hold healing properties, providing medicine for God's people. Amazing! Forever, the Israelites will remain strong and healthy, having been provided with good nutrition and natural medicine. As in Eden, their lifestyle will be fully organic, with no requirement for chemicals or processed substances – God will provide for His chosen ones out of the perfection of His creation. They need only to trust in Him. And forever they will sing praises of His goodness.

So Israel will grow to be beautiful and abundant. The Lord's life-giving water and vegetation will provide for His royal priesthood, in this great land of plenty.

Isaiah 41:18-20 – 'I will open rivers in desolate heights, and fountains in the midst of the valleys; I will make the wilderness a pool of water, and the dry land springs of water. I will plant in the wilderness the cedar and the acacia tree, the myrtle and the oil tree; I will set in the desert the cypress tree and the pine and the box tree together, that they may see and know, and consider and understand together, that the hand of the Lord has done this, and the Holy One of Israel has created it.'

It is the Holy One of Israel who will restore life to the Promised Land – life in great abundance. What was once desert land, will thrive with waters and trees of glorious variety. This spectacular land will be the home of the children of God!

Chapter 15

The Construction of Jerusalem

Jerusalem will be an incredible place during the Millennial Kingdom. It shall be the centre of God's holy nation, where Christ will dwell and reign from Zion. With excellency, He will rebuild His city into the image of majesty.

Isaiah 60:17-18 – "Instead of bronze I will bring gold, instead of iron I will bring silver, instead of wood, bronze, and instead of stones, iron. I will also make your officers peace, and your magistrates righteousness. Violence shall no longer be heard in your land, neither wasting nor destruction within your borders; but you shall call your walls Salvation, and your gates Praise."

Jerusalem shall be rebuilt with only the most precious and beautiful metals. Its buildings will be constructed with gold, silver, bronze and iron. Anything less valuable will be cast aside as unworthy. Officers and magistrates will be appointed over the land by Christ, and they will rule with peace and righteousness. Violence and destruction will never again be seen in all Israel, and war and wickedness will be no more. God's holy nation will be beautiful and full of righteousness.

The Lord will name Jerusalem's walls Salvation, and its gates, Praise! His royal priesthood will be exalted above all the nations of the earth, and His glory will radiate from the holy city. Christ, Israel's Salvation, will be a wall of protection around them, and the gates of Praise will be entered by those coming to worship the King of all kings.

As well as being called Praise, each gate will be named after a tribe of Israel:

Ezekiel 48:31 – "(the gates of the city shall be named after the tribes of Israel), the three gates northward: one gate for Reuben, one gate for Judah, and one gate for Levi".

This verse comes from a large passage (Ezekiel 40-48) describing Ezekiel's vision of the Millennial temple and city. It is a fascinating documentation, unveiling many incredible details. From the verse above, we can see that Jerusalem will have gates named after Reuben, Simeon, Levi, Judah, Issachar, Zebulun, Dan, Gad, Asher, Naphtali, Joseph, and Benjamin. There will be three gates on each four sides of the city – twelve in total. It was to Abraham, Isaac, and Jacob that the pledge of the Promised Land was first made to, and the names of these twelve descendants of theirs will be honoured in this land forever. Ezekiel 47-48 also mentions that the land will be divided into sections for each tribe of Israel, and that a portion will be given to each people. God's chosen ones will be gathered from the nations and joined to different tribes to settle in. Their given tribe will be theirs and their descendants' forever.

Ezekiel's vision continues on with more details:

Ezekiel 48:35 – "All the way around shall be eighteen thousand cubits; and the name of the city from that day shall be: THE LORD IS THERE."

Jerusalem will be called 'The Lord Is There'! Christ will rule among His people, His treasured possessions, for one thousand years. The bride and Bridegroom will dwell together, forever face to face, living in adoration and joy. All surrounding nations shall know that Jerusalem is the land of God, chosen by Him to rule from.

In regard to the measurement of eighteen thousand cubits, there seems to be some variation in conversion methods, producing results that range from four miles to thirty-four miles in circumference. Whatever the distance though, we know that this city will be full of abundant life, brimming with people and animals (as explored in the following chapter). Even outside of the city, God's children will make their homes, dwelling all throughout the land Israel.

More information is given on the borders and area of Jerusalem in Jeremiah:

Jeremiah 31:38-40 – "Behold, the days are coming, says the Lord, that the city shall be built for the Lord from the Tower of Hananel to the Corner Gate. The surveyor's line shall again extend straight forward over the hill Gareb; then it shall turn toward Goath. And the whole valley of the dead bodies and of the ashes, and all the fields as far as the Brook Kidron, to the corner of the Horse Gate toward the east, shall be holy to the Lord. It shall not be plucked up or thrown down anymore forever."

It is amazing to think that God has already planned out every detail of His Millennial Kingdom city. Locations and constructions have been perfectly designed by the Creator of all, ready for the day of Israel's great restoration. When Christ rebuilds His city, its boundaries will extend further than before, reaching new landmarks. The Tower of Hananel (literally meaning 'God's grace') and the Corner Gate were part of the original perimeter of Jerusalem, standing alongside its border. However, Goath and the hill of Gareb will be new expansions of the city, increasing its size. And the valley of dead bodies, which once lay outside Jerusalem, will now be called holy, representing the transformation of death to life among the land of Israel. What was once kept outside as unclean will be cleansed by Christ, and joined to His wonderous city. All the land of Jerusalem will stay holy forever, set apart for the Lord and for His children, as the inheritance promised to their forefathers. And never again will the Lord scatter Israel throughout the nations. With new hearts of flesh, God's chosen ones will remain obedient to the Lord, abiding in His ways and receiving His blessings.

They will serve Christ, and He will protect them.

Zechariah 2:4b-5 – 'Jerusalem shall be inhabited as towns without walls, because of the multitude of men and livestock in it. For I,' says the Lord, 'will be a wall of fire all around her, and I will be the glory in her midst.'

Christ will be a wall of fire around His people! He will be great and glorious in Her midst! Physical walls would only limit the expansion of His holy city and the movement of His people. They would not be able to contain the abundance of men and livestock that will dwell in its streets! And Jerusalem will not need physical walls to protect themselves from enemies – Christ Himself will be a shield for His people against attack, guarding the city on all sides with His mighty fire. For the walls will be called Salvation (**Isaiah 60:18**), and Salvation amazingly translates in Hebrew to Yeshua (Jesus), meaning 'Yahweh saves'. Yeshua is our refuge and our strength. God, our Consuming Fire, will surround us with His marvellous presence. What power! What furious protection! Forever, He will be the glory in the midst of Israel.

Chapter 16

The Inhabitants of The Land

Jerusalem will be such a wonderful city, and young and old will make their home in its streets. We, the Bride of Christ, will live in unity, in the city that the Lord has built up from ruins, and restored into a glory unlike anything ever seen.

Zechariah 8:4-6 – "Thus says the Lord of hosts: 'Old men and old women shall again sit in the streets of Jerusalem, each one with his staff in his hand because of great age. The streets of the city shall be full of boys and girls playing in its streets.' Thus says the Lord of hosts: 'If it is marvellous in the eyes of the remnant of this people in these days, will it also be marvellous in My eyes?' Says the Lord of hosts."

The Lord's city will be full of great life and joy. Young boys and girls will play in the streets, with no fear of being harmed. Their freedom will be unparalleled, and Christ will take delight in their pleasure. The presence of young children in Jerusalem provides evidence for continued family life and reproduction throughout the Millennial Kingdom. People will marry, have children, grow old and die as before – but their lives will be so much more glorious and their land so much more beautiful than now. Marriage and birth will continue among mankind until a new heaven and a new earth are created, and the second resurrection takes place (**Mark 12:25**). Only those who were martyred before Christ's return to earth, and have risen to reign with Him for the thousand years, will neither reproduce nor die again in this period (**Revelation 20:4**).

As well as young children, the elderly will also commune in the streets of Jerusalem, sitting with one another. The mention of a staff in their hand gives the idea that people in the Millennial Kingdom will grow to ages greater than today's normal. Nowadays, we might see seventy to eighty-year-olds walking with sticks, but it is hard to imagine they would require this support during Christ's reign, living in a land of such abundance and healing. Perhaps, because Israel will live in the presence of God, surrounded by His healing nature, they will live to the ages of pre-flood Bible times. That would explain the need for staffs! Adam lived to nine-hundred-and-thirty years (**Genesis 5:5**), and Methuselah, the oldest person that ever lived, died at nine-hundred-and-sixty-nine years (**Genesis 5:27**)! If people lived to these ages when the world was still corrupt and full of sin, how much more likely is it that people will reach these ages in a holy nation, where their Saviour dwells with them? After all, who would wish to have a short life in the Millennial Kingdom? That would be terrible! People will desire to live in Jerusalem with Christ for hundreds of years. Even so, they will know that after death, there is hope of living with the Lord throughout eternal life.

In the Millennial Kingdom, God will bless His holy nation with health and long life, with both young and old inhabiting Jerusalem together. It will be marvellous in both the eyes of God and His people. And animals too, will dwell together in perfect peace and harmony.

Isaiah 11:6-9 – "The wolf also shall dwell with the lamb, the leopard shall lie down with the young goat, the calf and the young lion and the fatling together; and a little child shall lead them. The cow and the bear shall graze; their young ones shall lie down together; and the lion shall eat straw like the ox. The nursing child shall play by the cobra's hole, and the weaned child shall put his hand in the viper's den. They shall not hurt nor destroy in all My holy mountain, for the earth shall be full of the knowledge of the Lord as the waters cover the sea."

In the years of the Millennial Kingdom, there will be absolute peace between all species of animals. They will become herbivores, no longer hunting each other, but dwelling together in friendship and harmony. The bears and lions, once predator animals, will graze on grass and straw like cows. We can surmise that God will change their digestive systems, allowing them to become satisfied on forage alone, rather than the flesh of other animals. Just as humans will no longer kill each other in battle, so will an end be put to animals hunting one another. God's peace will be restored among creation. The wolves and leopards will dwell with the lambs and young goats, with not a thought of violence toward the young, but only that of care and enjoyment of their presence. All animal young will lie together at rest and at calm. Israel will be changed into an Eden-like paradise, and it will remain as such for one thousand years.

This is such an incredible and unusual picture - so much so, that one may think it is referring to eternal life, rather than describing earth during Christ's reign. But we know it is the Millennial Kingdom being talked of here, because the verses afterward (Isaiah 11:10-12) say that this description takes place on the day Christ will bring His people back to Israel. This land full of peace and freedom from fear is the inheritance that He is calling His chosen ones back to. The Lord will restore to earth His original plan for mankind.

Not only will there be perfect harmony between different types of animals, but also between animals and humans. Young children will play peaceably with all kinds of animals without any fear or danger. Infants will entertain themselves with cobras and vipers, putting their hands in dens without fear of bites or venom. They will lead the lion and fatling, involving them in their play. All across God's holy mountain, and throughout His chosen nation, not one animal shall hurt or destroy. Humans and animals, both of which were originally created to bring glory to the Lord, will proclaim His excellencies in word and action.

Zechariah 14:20a – 'In that day "HOLINESS TO THE Lord" shall be engraved on the bells of the horses.'

It is likely that in these days, transport will come from horses instead of motor vehicles. And, in the Millennial Kingdom, all animals shall be under the possession of Christ, having His name and praises written upon themselves. Wherever these horses walk, bells will chime praises to the Most High King. Holiness to the Lord will be proclaimed all throughout the land!

And all the people too, will praise the Lord with joy.

Jeremiah 31:23-25 – 'Thus says the Lord of hosts, the God of Israel: "They shall again use this speech in the land of Judah and in its cities, when I bring back their captivity: 'The Lord bless you, O home of justice, and mountain of holiness!' And there shall dwell in Judah itself, and in all its cities together, farmers and those going out with flocks. For I have satiated the weary soul, and I have replenished every sorrowful soul.'"

When God's people are gathered from the wicked nations of the earth, and brought back to this glorious new city, they will bless this land of their inheritance in the name of the Lord. With praise and thanksgiving, they shall enter the gates and courts of King Jesus. For they have arrived at the land of justice and holiness! Those who are weary and sorrowful will be satiated and replenished with the glory of God, entering the 'cities' (for there will be more than one city in Israel) of God at peace. Farmers will be at rest in the land that God has provided for them, living among other children of God with their flocks and herds, dwelling in cities and countryside alike.

The whole of Israel will be joyful in praise, coming together from many nations to be with their King.

Isaiah 66:6 – 'The sound of noise from the city! A voice from the temple! The voice of the Lord, who fully repays His enemies!'

There will be a great noise from Jerusalem when the remnant of Israel join together in the Promised Land. A triumphant shout will fill the city! People will celebrate like never before, at home with their Saviour. Their enemies will be defeated on all sides, and the temple will once again resound with praise and worship to the Lord of all.

Chapter 17

Christ's Temple

In Jerusalem, Christ shall rebuild His temple upon Mount Zion, where He will rule for one thousand years. With righteousness and truth, He will judge the nations, and the temple will radiate with His glory.

Zechariah 1:16-17 – 'Therefore thus says the Lord: "I am returning to Jerusalem with mercy; My house shall be built in it," says the Lord of hosts, "And a surveyor's line shall be stretched out over Jerusalem." Again proclaim, saying, 'Thus says the Lord of hosts: "My cities shall again spread out through prosperity; The Lord will again comfort Zion, and will again choose Jerusalem."'

Upon the Lord's return, Christ will again choose Jerusalem as His home, and build His house upon Mount Zion. The surveyor's line will be spread over the land, and the temple and cities shall be rebuilt, blessed with prosperity and favour from the Lord. After having dispersed Israel throughout the nations due to their rebellion, He will lead the faithful ones back home to dwell with Himself, and treat them as His special possessions. Christ will comfort His people, showing them great mercy, forgiving them of their iniquity and bringing them great joy.

His temple too will be made glorious and beautiful.

Haggai 2:6-9 – "For thus says the Lord of hosts: 'Once more (it is a little while) I will shake heaven and earth, the sea and dry land; and I will shake all nations, and they shall come to the Desire of All Nations, and I will fill this temple with glory,' says the Lord of hosts. 'The silver is Mine, and the gold is Mine,' says the Lord of hosts. 'The glory of this latter temple shall be greater than the former,' says the Lord of hosts. 'And in this place I will give peace,' says the Lord of hosts."

It will be after the shaking of the nations during the end times tribulation, that the Lord's children will be brought back to the Promised Land, the Desire of All Nations. All the riches of this world belong to Jesus - the Lord of lords and King of kings. With gold and silver He will build up His new temple to be even more glorious than the former two (the temple built by Solomon, and the rebuilt temple after Israel's exile to Babylon). From this new temple, our mighty Prince will establish peace throughout all nations. The shakings of the world will come to an end, and for one thousand years, the earth will be filled with the knowledge of God's glory. Christ's temple will be spectacular, and His rule wonderful.

Isaiah 2:2-3 – 'Now it shall come to pass in the latter days that the mountain of the Lord's house shall be established on the top of the mountains, and shall be exalted above the hills; and all nations shall flow to it. Many people shall come and say, "Come, and let us go up to the mountain of the Lord, to the house of the God of Jacob; He will teach us His ways, and we shall walk in His paths." For out of Zion shall go forth the law, and the word of the Lord from Jerusalem.'

The Lord's temple will be exalted high upon the hill of Zion, and all will come to worship Him there – people from every tribe and nation will come and bow before His throne. Christ will teach

His ways to all, and they shall walk in His paths, remaining obedient to His word and law. All the earth shall seek the wisdom of the Lord of heaven and earth, desiring to meet with Him face to face in Jerusalem. How marvellous this will be! And Christ our Redeemer will live in unchallenged authority. All will worship before the King of Israel and bring offerings to His holy temple.

Ezekiel 20:40-41 – "'For on My holy mountain, on the mountain height of Israel," says the Lord God, "there all the house of Israel, all of them in the land, shall serve Me; there I will accept them, and there I will require your offerings and the firstfruits of your sacrifices, together with all your holy things. I will accept you as a sweet aroma when I bring you out from the peoples and gather you out of the countries where you have been scattered; and I will be hallowed in you before the Gentiles.'"

All throughout the land of Israel, God's children will serve Him faithfully. They have been bought and purified by the blood of the Lamb, and will become His royal priests. Serving Christ will be their one mission, as it should be for us now. It is interesting that with the return of the temple, offerings and sacrifices to the Lord will be resumed. We will give God all our 'holy things' and He will accept our offerings as pleasing to Him. When the remnant of Israel return to their land, the Lord will restore holiness and purity to His people. And in this day, Isael will be a sweet aroma to their Bridegroom King.

Malachi 3:4 – "Then the offering of Judah and Jerusalem Will be pleasant to the Lord, as in the days of old, as in former years."

Malachi reiterates the pleasure that the Lord will receive from Israel's offerings, in the days of the elect's return. Just as in the days of old, Israel shall be His holy nation, and He will be their

God. This time though, the Lord's presence will not be concealed in the holy of holies, resting between the two cherubim of the tabernacle, but Christ will rule and reign in the temple for all to see.

In Ezekiel 45 and 46, we see that the sabbath, the new moons, and the Passover will be celebrated at the temple, as well as other feasts and offerings. These holy celebrations will continue throughout the Millennial Kingdom, as in former years.

Ezekiel 45:21-22 – "In the first month, on the fourteenth day of the month, you shall observe the Passover, a feast of seven days; unleavened bread shall be eaten. And on that day the prince shall prepare for himself and for all the people of the land a bull for a sin offering."

Ezekiel 46:3-5 – "Likewise the people of the land shall worship at the entrance to this gateway before the Lord on the Sabbaths and the New Moons. The burnt offering that the prince offers to the Lord on the Sabbath day shall be six lambs without blemish, and a ram without blemish; and the grain offering shall be one ephah for a ram, and the grain offering for the lambs, as much as he wants to give, as well as a hin of oil with every ephah."

There is great detail within these chapters describing how these feasts, offerings and sacrifices are to be carried out, and what is required for each one. It is a written manual for the resumption of worship at the temple when Christ rules on earth. People will take part in Passover to remember that the Lord has delivered them from their enemies, just as He brought the Israelites out of Egypt in the days of Moses. The Feast of Tabernacles will be remembered (Zechariah 14:16) to celebrate how He is now residing with His people and providing for them, just as He resided with the Israelites and provided for them after they passed through the Red Sea and into the wilderness. As well as these set times, holy days such as sabbaths and new moons will also be observed. On these special occasions, everyone from the land of Israel will come to the gates of the temple, and worship before Christ Jesus the King. Not only is He their Shepherd and Bridegroom, but He is also their Lord, worthy of fear and reverence from all mankind. Every generation will worship Him with holy offerings, and it will be to Him as a sweet aroma.

And in the Millennial Kingdom, within the land of Israel, what was once classified as common will be made holy in the presence of God.

Zechariah 14:20 – 'In that day "HOLINESS TO THE Lord" shall be engraved on the bells of the horses. The pots in the Lord's house shall be like the bowls before the altar.'

Even the horses will declare the holiness of God! There will not be a living thing exempt from praising their Creator. All the pots in the temple of God will be as holy as the ones used upon the altar for sacrifices. Israel will be a land of inescapable beauty and glory, because of the extent of its holiness.

And the majesty of God will not just remain in His temple, but will spread out throughout the land, bringing healing and life to all. Rushing water shall flow out from the temple, as seen in Ezekiel's vision:

Ezekiel 47:1-2 – 'Then he brought me back to the door of the   temple; and there was water, flowing from under the threshold of the temple toward the east, for the front of the temple faced east; the water was flowing from under the right side of the temple, south of the altar.   He brought me out by way of the north gate, and led me around on the outside to the outer gateway that faces east; and there was water, running out on the right side.'

In this vision, an angel shows Ezekiel a river of living water, flowing from under the right side of the temple, and gushing towards the east. This water will flow from the temple where Christ's rule is established - the most holy place in Jerusalem. As discussed in chapter 14, this is the same river that will restore life to all living things, and have healing trees growing upon its riverbanks. When people worship Christ in His temple, it will give way for blessings to be released across the nation of Israel, bringing living waters to the land. When we make Christ King in our lives, He fills us with His Spirit of life and freedom.

His presence will be upon all people.

Isaiah 4:5-6 – 'then the Lord will create above every dwelling place of Mount Zion, and above her assemblies, a cloud and smoke by day and the shining of a flaming fire by night. For over all the glory there will be a covering. And there will be a tabernacle for shade in the daytime from the heat, for a place of refuge, and for a shelter from storm and rain.'

As in the days of Exodus, when Israel wondered across the desert in wait of the Promised Land, a cloud of smoke by day and a flame of fire by night will once again guide and comfort God's people. What an awesome sight this will be! The children of God will not have to enter the temple of the Lord in order to be with Christ – forever, He will completely encompass them with His powerful, holy presence. Christ will be the glory in the midst of Israel. And the Lord will provide for His people shelter and refuge in the form of a tabernacle in Jerusalem. It will be for them a cool shade in the heat of day, and a dry and comforting place to rest in the midst of storm and rain. Fear shall not take hold of the holy ones of Israel, nor shall they ever be separated from the glorious presence of Christ.

Earlier on in Ezekiel's vision, the Millennial Temple is revealed in detail. It is a place filled with the awesome majesty and splendour of the Lord, to an extent that would make any onlooker tremble with wonder.

Ezekiel 43:1-9 – 'Afterward he brought me to the gate, the gate that faces toward the east. And behold, the glory of the God of Israel came from the way of the east. His voice was like the sound of many waters; and the earth shone with His glory. It was like the appearance of the vision which I saw—like the vision which I saw when I came to destroy the city. The visions were like the vision which I saw by the River Chebar; and I fell on my face. And the glory of the Lord came into the temple by way of the gate which faces toward the east. The Spirit lifted me up and brought me into the inner court; and behold, the glory of the Lord filled the temple.

Then I heard Him speaking to me from the temple, while a man stood beside me. And He said to me, "Son of man, this is the place of My throne and the place of the soles of My feet, where I will dwell in the midst of the children of Israel forever. No more shall the house of Israel defile My holy name, they nor their kings, by their harlotry or with the carcasses of their kings on their high places. When they set their threshold by My threshold, and their doorpost by My doorpost, with a wall between them and Me, they defiled My holy name by the abominations which they committed; therefore I have consumed them in My anger. Now let them put their harlotry and the carcasses of their kings far away from Me, and I will dwell in their midst forever.'

Wow! What a picture! The King of glory, too majestic for words, will really rule on earth - the very earth we are living on! And from His third temple, He will govern the nations. When Ezekiel was following the angel in His vision, He encountered the glory of God before He even walked through the gates. The voice of the Lord was like many waters and the whole earth shone with

His radiance. His glory filled the whole temple. At the sight of this, Ezekiel fell on His face, too weak and humbled to stand in the presence of the Almighty God.

It is from this temple that Christ will dwell in the midst of the children of Israel for the Millenium. The soles of His feet will rest here for one thousand years, and it is here that His throne will be built. No more will His name be defiled by the sins and disobedience of Israel - the elect shall turn to Christ with their whole hearts, worshipping Him in spirit and in truth. And when they turn away from their sins, Christ will return to them with joy, dwelling in their midst forever and purifying them as His holy nation. He will be their God and King, and they shall be His priests and servants.

Chapter 18

The Nations of the Earth

Christ's second coming will be a time of great hope for believers, but a time of fear for those who have not followed God.

Revelation 19:15 – 'Now out of His mouth goes a sharp sword, that with it He should strike the nations. And He Himself will rule them with a rod of iron. He Himself treads the winepress of the fierceness and wrath of Almighty God.'

The Messiah will return with great vengeance, devouring enemies in His wrath. Those outside of Israel, who remain in other nations, will come under His fierce rule. Some who were oppressors of God's people will be taken captive by Israel, becoming their servants.

Isaiah 14:1-2 – 'For the Lord will have mercy on Jacob, and will still choose Israel, and settle them in their own land. The strangers will be joined with them, and they will cling to the house of Jacob. Then people will take them and bring them to their place, and the house of Israel will possess them for servants and maids in the land of the Lord; they will take them captive whose captives they were, and rule over their oppressors.'

In His mercy, God will settle His elect back into the Promised Land, and strangers will be joined to them. The Lord will once again choose Israel as a nation for His own possession, to bless and to prosper. From this land, Israel shall rule over their oppressors, taking captive those whose captives they were. People from other nations will be drawn to Israel, becoming servants and maids of the Lord's people. Once, they exalted themselves at the expense of God's children, but now, they shall be humbled. All the while, Israel will be greatly exalted by the hand of their King.

Isaiah 49:23 – "Kings shall be your foster fathers, and their queens your nursing mothers; they shall bow down to you with their faces to the earth, and lick up the dust of your feet. Then you will know that I am the Lord, for they shall not be ashamed who wait for Me."

Even former kings and queens will serve God's people, humbling themselves before the Lord's bride. They will nurse Israel's young and lick the dust at their feet. These wicked nations will spend their lives at service to Israel and their God, and the world will know that Yahweh is Lord. But those who wait upon the Lord will indeed renew their strength! They will never be brought to shame, but will soar above the nations of the earth on wings like eagles (Isaiah 40:31).

And all who are left among the nations will live a life of worship to Christ the King.

Zechariah 14:16-18 – 'And it shall come to pass that everyone who is left of all the nations which came against Jerusalem shall go up from year to year to worship the King, the Lord of hosts, and to keep the Feast of Tabernacles. And it shall be that whichever of the families of the earth do not come up to Jerusalem to worship the King, the Lord of hosts, on them there will be no rain. If the family of Egypt will not come up and enter in, they shall have no rain; they shall receive the plague with which the Lord strikes the nations who do not come up to keep the Feast of Tabernacles.'

Each year, those living in other nations will enter the city of Jerusalem to celebrate the Feast of Tabernacles with Israel. They will come to worship Jesus, the King of kings, giving Him adoration and praise! Whole families will go to Israel together, leaving no one behind. However, anyone who does not keep the Feast of Tabernacles will receive due punishment from God. No rain will fall on their land, causing it to be troubled with drought, and their soils will become unproductive and barren. As has always been the case, curses come to those who disobey God, and upon those who do not fear His name.

However, it will not just be out of requirement that nations will come to worship before the Lord – people will find it a delight to be in the presence of His majesty!

Zechariah 8:21-23 – 'The inhabitants of one city shall go to another, saying, "Let us continue to go and pray before the Lord, and seek the Lord of hosts. I myself will go also." Yes, many peoples and strong nations shall come to seek the Lord of hosts in Jerusalem, and to pray before the Lord. Thus says the Lord of hosts: 'In those days ten men from every language of the nations shall grasp the sleeve of a Jewish man, saying, "Let us go with you, for we have heard that God is with you."'

Inhabitants from cities all across the world will eagerly ask one another to travel to Israel. They will desire to go and seek the Lord, longing to pray before Him. Christ will be the treasure of all nations – in His presence there is fullness of joy, and at His right hand are pleasures forevermore (Psalm 16:11). Both the strong and weak alike will come and worship before the King of kings, travelling huge distances to kneel before His throne. It is stated here that at least ten men from each nation will grasp the sleeve of an Israelite man, longing to enter Jerusalem with him! Those living in Israel will be envied by all nations - everyone will hear that the Lord is with them and has chosen them as His own.

Israel will be greatly blessed by their God, and they will become the beauty of the earth. For the glory of God will dwell in their midst, and all the earth will hunger to be near Jesus Christ.

Isaiah 2:4 – 'He shall judge between the nations, and rebuke many people; they shall beat their swords into ploughshares, and their spears into pruning hooks; nation shall not lift up sword against nation, neither shall they learn war anymore.'

From His holy temple, Christ will judge the nations, solving disputes with perfect justice and rebuking what is wrong. People will come from far countries to hear His judgements, and will be amazed at His wisdom and authority. In His ability to solve disputes, our Prince of Peace will put an end to war among the nations for one thousand years! Their swords and spears will be remoulded into tools used for agricultural production. Instead of decreased life due to battle, there will be an increase of life due to abundant food. And all will be content and calm – the one that is out to kill, steal and destroy, is safely locked away in the bottomless pit.

After the first wars against Israel's enemies at the return of Christ, there will be no need for more. All remaining people will submit to God's chosen nation, in humbleness and holy fear.

Isaiah 60:14 – "Also the sons of those who afflicted you shall come bowing to you, and all those who despised you shall fall prostrate at the soles of your feet; and they shall call you The City of the Lord, Zion of the Holy One of Israel."

People who once despised and afflicted believers in Christ, will come bowing down to them, prostrate at their feet. This is quite an image! God will turn all things around for the good of those who love Him. For no weapon formed against His children will prosper - it will fire back at the very people who took the shot.

114

The nations of the earth shall call Israel 'The City of the Lord' and 'Zion of the Holy One of Israel'. All the earth will acknowledge that the Lord is with His people! They will realise their foolishness in having rejected Christ, and will be filled with remorse over their wickedness. In awe, they will stand amazed at the glory of the Lord, and what He has done for His people, Israel.

Isaiah 55:5 – "Surely you shall call a nation you do not know, and nations who do not know you shall run to you, because of the Lord your God, and the Holy One of Israel; for He has glorified you."

Israel will be able to call on foreign nations, receiving help from other countries because of how God has blessed them. The Lord has glorified and strengthened them, upholding Israel with His righteous right hand - Jesus (Isaiah 41:10). Foreign nations will run to them, overwhelmed by a desire to be in the presence of the Lord's chosen people, and with Christ Himself. Israel will be blessed by those who once afflicted them.

Isaiah 60:11 – "Therefore your gates shall be open continually; they shall not be shut day or night, that men may bring to you the wealth of the Gentiles, and their kings in procession."

Jerusalem's gates will be open continually, allowing for multitudes of people to enter the city, day and night. Men from many nations will come into the holy city to give their wealth to the children of the Lord. Even kings will bring their gifts, entering through the gates in procession. God's chosen nation will be abundantly blessed by all those surrounding them. Christ will glorify Israel and will prosper them in His presence.

Isaiah 60:5-7 – "Then you shall see and become radiant, and your heart shall swell with joy; because the abundance of the sea shall be turned to you, the wealth of the Gentiles shall come to you. The multitude of camels shall cover your land, the dromedaries of Midian and Ephah; all those from Sheba shall come; they shall bring gold and incense, and they shall proclaim the praises of the Lord. All the flocks of Kedar shall be gathered together to you, the rams of Nebaioth shall minister to you; they shall ascend with acceptance on My altar, and I will glorify the house of My glory."

All Israel will become radiant with joy, their hearts swelling with delight! God will restore to them one hundredfold of what was lost in captivity. The wealth of the Gentiles will be turned to them, and riches in abundance will arrive at their shores. Multitudes of camels and flocks will be given to Israel, filling their land with life and food. Gold and incense will be brought to them, increasing their wealth and beauty. For all nations will bless the children of the Lord and proclaim praises to the King!

God's promises to Abraham, Isaac and Jacob will be fulfilled. The Lord's chosen race, the people for His own possession, will return to the Promised Land, where they will be cleansed and abundantly blessed. Israel will be glorified by their Redeemer and Saviour, Yeshua HaMashiach.

Chapter 19

Promises to Remember

The Millennial Kingdom will be a magnificent time in the future, and we should look forward to it with great eagerness! Although we do not yet know the hour in which Christ will return, we can see that the seasons are currently changing in preparation for His arrival (Matthew 24). Therefore, we should be on guard and stay awake, so that He does not come to us as a thief in the night, unexpectedly (Revelation 16:5). We need to remain in God, reading His word, praying, worshipping, and making disciples of all nations. We need to learn to recognise the Lord's voice and to obey it at all costs. When Christ returns, He is not coming back for a group of lukewarm Christians, but for a pure and spotless bride, ready for marriage to her Saviour King (Ephesians 5:25-27).

If we seek wisdom from the Lord, and fear His name, God tells us that He will reveal unknown secrets to us (Psalm 25:14). The Holy Spirit will guide us in all wisdom, and once overlooked Bible passages will become alive and full of meaning to us. We should hold tightly to the promises embedded within God's word, and allow it to bubble up hope within us, reviving our souls. Our hope is in the things not yet seen, giving us the perseverance to endure this life for what is to come (Romans 8:24-25). For our God is with us, and He loves us. We should never be afraid of the trials of this life, but should stand firm in Christ our Salvation through it all.

In Revelation, Jesus speaks to John in a vision, revealing to Him the rewards given to those 'who overcome', just as Christ Himself overcame in this world. Overcomers are those who live righteously and in faith, according to the will of the Father, whilst throwing off the temptations of sin. It is written in 1 John 5:4: 'For whatever is born of God overcomes the world. And this is the victory that has overcome the world—our faith.' It is our faith in Christ, and the power of God within us, that will allow us to overcome the spirit of the antichrist in the last days (1 John 4:3-4). And those who overcome until the end, remaining close to God, will be greatly blessed.

Whilst a few of these promises given by Jesus in Revelation will take place during the Millennial Kingdom, many of them will take place at the time of, or after, the second resurrection (which happens on the day of judgement, when eternity begins). Not all believers will be alive during the period of the Millennial Kingdom, but those that do not experience it will receive their reward in eternity. New Jerusalem, God's eternal kingdom (discussed in the following chapter) will see many of Christ's words fulfilled.

Below is a collection of beautiful promises to treasure and to keep:

Revelation 2:7b – "To him who overcomes I will give to eat from the tree of life, which is in the midst of the Paradise of God."

If we overcome, the same tree that was in the Garden of Eden will be made available to us! We will eat of its life-giving fruits and live forevermore with our God.

Revelation 2:11b – "He who overcomes shall not be hurt by the second death."

If we overcome, we will not be subject to the second death – that is, the casting of souls into the lake of fire (**Revelation 20:14-15**).

Revelation 2:17b – "To him who overcomes I will give some of the hidden manna to eat. And I will give him a white stone, and on the stone a new name written which no one knows except him who receives it."

If we overcome, God will give us hidden manna to eat – the very food of angels (**Psalm 78:25**)! Each of us will be given a white stone, representing purity, and be given a new name by God, personal and secret to each of us.

Revelation 2:26-28 – "And he who overcomes, and keeps My works until the end, to him I will give power over the nations— 'He shall rule them with a rod of iron; They shall be dashed to pieces like the potter's vessels'— as I also have received from My Father; and I will give him the morning star."

If we overcome, we will have power over the nations, ruling with the Messiah and defeating our enemies. We will be given the Morning Star – a term often used in scripture to describe Jesus Himself. Forever we will be with our Lord.

Revelation 3:5 – "He who overcomes shall be clothed in white garments, and I will not blot out his name from the Book of Life; but I will confess his name before My Father and before His angels."

If we overcome, our names will remain written in the Book of Life, and we will live forever! The Lord will clothe us in white - the blood of the Lamb has purified us and made us holy. And Christ will confess and acknowledge us before the Father and His angels! If we confess Him before men on earth, He promises to confess us before His Father in heaven (Matthew 10:32).

Revelation 3:12 – "He who overcomes, I will make him a pillar in the temple of My God, and he shall go out no more. I will write on him the name of My God and the name of the city of My God, the New Jerusalem, which comes down out of heaven from My God. And I will write on him My new name."

If we overcome, we will become a pillar in the temple of God, supporting His kingdom and abiding in His dwelling place. We will strengthen ourselves in His presence and never be cast away! The Lord will write His name upon us, even His new name, as well as the name of New Jerusalem. We will belong to Him and His Kingdom forevermore.

Revelation 3:21 – "To him who overcomes I will grant to sit with Me on My throne, as I also overcame and sat down with My Father on His throne."

If we overcome, we will be granted to sit on Christ's throne with Him! Just as He sat on His Father's throne when He Himself overcame the world! Christ will exalt us, dressing us with His own righteousness and glory.

Revelation 21:7 – "He who overcomes shall inherit all things, and I will be his God and he shall be My son."

If we overcome, we will inherit all things – we are adopted into God's family and will be given access to all of His creation! We are, and will eternally be, the children of the one, true, living God!

What magnificent promises these are! Hallelujah!! How could we humans, wicked in our nature, and created from dust, be blessed with such excellencies? It is only by the blood of the Lamb that we are able to receive such delightful wonders. It is only through Christ's death on the cross that we are healed from the curse of sin and brought into new life with the Father. The glorious treasures ahead of us almost make our current trials seem laughable. If we can overcome them and remain close to God, we will be blessed with some of the greatest promises ever given to mankind.

Therefore, we must continue to abide in Christ and walk in His statutes. The convenience of living like this world is not worth losing our glorious inheritance over! Our birthright must not be sold for things that only satisfy the body and then are gone (**Genesis 25**). We need to live lives according to our identity as God's royal priesthood, chosen and anointed to serve Him all our days! Our mission should be to see His kingdom come and His will to be done, on earth just as in heaven (**Matthew 6:10**). We need to prepare ourselves to become Christ's pure and spotless bride, ready for our coming King!

Chapter 20

New Jerusalem

The one-thousand-year reign of Christ will be the most spectacular time that the world has ever witnessed. But just like all other millennials, it too will pass. Satan will be released for a short while, and then he and his armies will be destroyed in a lake of fire. All dead will resurrect for the day of judgement, and either rise to glorious new life in Christ, or be thrown into the lake of fire with Satan. We are told that the old heaven and earth will pass away and that new ones will be created.

Creation will start afresh, full of people who love the Lord dwelling face to face with their God and Maker. They will have transformed, glorious bodies, and will not reproduce further, but will each one live eternally. A New Jerusalem will descend to earth from heaven, more stunning than ever before. Forever, this glorious city will be the home of the Lord's chosen ones.

Revelation 21 and Revelation 22:1-5 beautifully describe what God has prepared for those who love Him:

'All Things Made New

Now I saw a new heaven and a new earth, for the first heaven and the first earth had passed away. Also there was no more sea. Then I, John, saw the holy city, New Jerusalem, coming down out of heaven from God, prepared as a bride adorned for her husband. And I heard a loud voice from heaven saying, "Behold, the tabernacle of God is with men, and He will dwell with them, and they shall be His people. God Himself will be with them and be their God. And God will wipe away every tear from their eyes; there shall be no more death, nor sorrow, nor crying. There shall be no more pain, for the former things have passed away."

Then He who sat on the throne said, "Behold, I make all things new." And He said to me, "Write, for these words are true and faithful."

And He said to me, "It is done! I am the Alpha and the Omega, the Beginning and the End. I will give of the fountain of the water of life freely to him who thirsts. He who overcomes shall inherit all things, and I will be his God and he shall be My son. But the cowardly, unbelieving, abominable, murderers, sexually immoral, sorcerers, idolaters, and all liars shall have their part in the lake which burns with fire and brimstone, which is the second death."

The New Jerusalem

Then one of the seven angels who had the seven bowls filled with the seven last plagues came to me and talked with me, saying, "Come, I will show you the bride, the Lamb's wife." And he carried me away in the Spirit to a great and high mountain, and showed me the great city, the holy Jerusalem, descending out of heaven from God, having the glory of God. Her light was like a most precious stone, like a jasper stone, clear as crystal. Also she had a great and high wall with twelve gates, and twelve angels at the gates, and names written on them, which are the names of the twelve tribes of the children of Israel: three gates on the east, three gates on the north, three gates on the south, and three gates on the west.

Now the wall of the city had twelve foundations, and on them were the names of the twelve apostles of the Lamb. And he who talked with me had a gold reed to measure the city, its gates, and its wall. The city is laid out as a square; its length is as great as its breadth. And he measured the city with the reed: twelve thousand furlongs.

Its length, breadth, and height are equal. Then he measured its wall: one hundred and forty-four cubits, according to the measure of a man, that is, of an angel. The construction of its wall was of jasper; and the city was pure gold, like clear glass. The foundations of the wall of the city were adorned with all kinds of precious stones: the first foundation was jasper, the second sapphire, the third chalcedony, the fourth emerald, the fifth sardonyx, the sixth sardius, the seventh chrysolite, the eighth beryl, the ninth topaz, the tenth chrysoprase, the eleventh jacinth, and the twelfth amethyst. The twelve gates were twelve pearls: each individual gate was of one pearl. And the street of the city was pure gold, like transparent glass.

The Glory of the New Jerusalem

But I saw no temple in it, for the Lord God Almighty and the Lamb are its temple. The city had no need of the sun or of the moon to shine in it, for the glory of God illuminated it. The Lamb is its light. And the nations of those who are saved shall walk in its light, and the kings of the earth bring their glory and honour into it. Its gates shall not be shut at all by day (there shall be no night there). And they shall bring the glory and the honour of the nations into it. But there shall by no means enter it anything that defiles, or causes an abomination or a lie, but only those who are written in the Lamb's Book of Life.

The River of Life

And he showed me a pure river of water of life, clear as crystal, proceeding from the throne of God and of the Lamb. In the middle of its street, and on either side of the river, was the tree of life, which bore twelve fruits, each tree yielding its fruit every month. The leaves of the tree were for the healing of the nations. And there shall be no more curse, but the throne of God and of the Lamb shall be in it, and His servants shall serve Him. They shall see His face, and His name shall be on their foreheads. There shall be no night there: They need no lamp nor light of the sun, for the Lord God gives them light. And they shall reign forever and ever.'

This, is the eternal inheritance of those who love the Lord! Let us rejoice exceedingly, and live a life worthy of the glory set before us. Thank you Yahweh, Yeshua and Holy Spirit!